Our Life in Dreams

TRIGUEIRINHO

Our Life in Dreams

Shasti Association

Copyright 2022 Shasti Association

Original Title in Portuguese
NOSSA VIDA NOS SONHOS
Copyright 1993 **José Trigueirinho Netto**

The profits generated from sales of books by Trigueirinho and his associates will be used to support the non-profit activities of the Shasti Association to disseminate their work

Translated by the Shasti Association translation team
Edited by Alan David Berkowitz (Micha-El) and
Magda Beatriz Rockett Berkowitz (Gran)

Cataloging-in-Publication Data

Trigueirinho Netto, José

Our Life in Dreams
Trigueirinho

Mount Shasta, CA, Shasti Association 2022 196 p.

ISBN: : 978-1-948430-13-5
Library of Congress Control Number: 2022943954

1. *Dreams*

2. *Spirituality*

3. *Self-Help*

I. *Title.*

English language rights reserved
P.O. Box 173
Mt. Shasta, CA 96067-0318
editorial@shasti.org
www.shasti.org

*Dedicated to the one Who
patiently instructed me.*

Contents

Publisher's Introduction	iii
Preface	v
An initial touch	1
Part I	5
The preparation	5
The importance of dreaming	7
Deep sleep and other types of dreams	23
Falling asleep correctly	35
Waking up correctly	45
The adventure of the night	51
Some cautions	63
Consequences of dreams	69
Common dreams and mental dreams	79
Teachings through dreams	93
The quality of dream life	101
Part II	109
Other steps	109
The spiritual function of dreams	111
The evolutionary dream	125
Dreams as messages of the soul	135

The reality beyond dreams	147
Prophetic dreams	153
A vision	159
Glossary	163
About Trigueirinho and his work	169
Books by Trigueirinho	173
Audios of Trigueirinho Lectures with simultaneous English translation	184

Publisher's introduction

Our Life in Dreams is a manual that teaches us how to open ourselves to dreams that take the form of messages from our deeper self, soul, or spirit. It is a book that clearly has an important message, with approximately 20 editions since it was originally published in Portuguese in 1993. The author teaches us that there are many different types of dreams that we can experience, often of a psychological origin, but that dreams can also give us messages from our higher self that provide spiritual guidance and that open us to deeper levels of reality. The book contains practical instructions about how to do this, with many powerful examples from the author's own life. It covers topics such as: the importance of dreams and the different types of dreams, how to fall asleep and how to wake up correctly, how dreams can connect us to higher levels of our being, and the different types of spiritual dreams that we can experience; including prophetic dreams, warning dreams, messages from our soul, and dreams of evolutionary significance. Unlike the more common dream books that focus on psychological themes and issues, this book offers us a pathway with specific techniques that allows us to use dreams as an important means of spiritual evolution, and helps us understand their deeper potentials and significance.

Preface

Our conscious life is need of an expansion of perspective, and for this, we do not require complex formulas that come from outside of us. We have an inner world, unexplored regions of our own consciousness, that need to be discovered. Moments of sleep are intrinsic to our human nature and not just a formality or something unusual. However, most of us do not value the state of sleep and consider it only as a physical rest, not realizing that during our time asleep, our consciousness transits through abstract dimensions that are also important elements of our experience, dimensions that represent experiences from another perspective. Human beings have many levels of consciousness and the vast majority of these are states and ways of expression that are different from the purely cerebral and concrete realities that are usually linked to our memories and previous experiences. We can see that our incarnation would be much broadened and that our learning would be increased if we accepted these realities and if we re-established an intimate, direct, simple relationship with them without intermediaries. Currently humanity is moving towards a cycle of liberation from limits, paradigms, and situations limited to its own personal karma. In this trajectory and in this current moment of transition we need more than ever to be open to other levels of consciousness so that we can, at the very least, accomplish a the broadening of our horizons and stimulate the long-awaited processes of purification that are happening to us. For this purpose, it is fundamental that we consider the moments of sleep as opportunities to contact other dimensions.

In this book, Trigueirinho leads us to awaken to such realities, stimulating us to undertake a beneficial and direct search for contact with our deeper levels. With instructions, examples and references, he helps us to rediscover treasures that are already within us. With the many impulses contained in this book, it will be up to each one of us to dedicate time and attention to rediscover what has always been within us, i.e., these internal levels which have been hidden from us due to our excessive and exclusive interest in the concrete level. Let us then, gratefully and without resistance, allow ourselves to wake up, becoming aware of the moments of sleep, which may include conscious or unconscious dreams, and to realize that we are always dreaming. In this way we have the opportunity to transit through existing levels of reality, contacting other dimensions that can complement our conscious life and provide us with an experience that is constructive, aware, more responsible and committed to our own evolution.

I wish for you all a good read.

About Friar Luciano

Friar Luciano is a consecrated monk of the Grace-Mercy Order, the General Secretary of the Fraternity International Humanitarian Foundation, and a member of its Permanent Guidance Council (*https://www.fraterinternacional.org/*). He works extensively with international humanitarian organizations, including the United Nations, and was a close personal collaborator of José Trigueirinho Neto. To learn more about Friar Luciano and his work, including recordings of his lectures with English translation, go to *https://www.freiluciano.org/*.

An initial touch

> *"A finger is used to point to the Moon;*
> *the wise look at the Moon,*
> *the ignorant at the finger."*
>
> Zen Proverb

This book is simply a finger that points towards something much larger. It contains basic and simple indications that may be of use, if you wish, in your process of development.

In the evolution of an individual, there are stages in which the transformations are slower. This can often be explained as a result of the compromises and concessions that we make to the older part of our being. However, there are also periods in which rapid changes are taking place and dreams may be valuable in the preparation for them.

At times, a dream repeats itself precisely in order for us to devote the necessary attention to it; the very fact that it is repeated means that it would be good to re-examine it, because it contains a special lesson. It may happen also that we have studied it but not in all the details. In this case, its message comes back in the form of a new dream or even of a recollection in order for us to have the opportunity to observe what has not yet been perceived by us. If a dream refers to a transformation that is occurring over a longer time, it can bring help to us in different stages of our journey.

In short, dreams constitute powerful allies of the evolution of humanity, and through them we are capable of participating in life at various levels of reality and consciousness.

A series of meetings that I held during the course of a year on this theme were recorded on tape. Then Maria Dagmar Bastos de Paula and other collaborators lovingly transcribed and organized this extensive recorded material, making it possible for me to work with it efficiently. Vanda de Oliveira Bittencourt contributed to the final revision of the first edition. Without this impulse, as well as that of the editor, I would not have been able to share my experience on this topic. Additions have been made to the original tapes, especially in the second part of the book, which was almost completely rewritten during the time in retreat when I was focused on the elaboration of the text.

Over the course of successive editions we were able to notice that the contents, because of their simplicity and above all, due to their being based on lived experience, were able to meet a necessity. The book was well-received in diverse areas of society, stimulating in many people a considerable impulse for knowledge of the inner world. Considering its utility, it was revised for the present edition, by updating the material and adding a comprehensive index. We hope that as a result of this new edition, the reader will come even more close to this subject, which shows itself to be so deep and so relevant today as it was at the time of its original release a few years ago.

Part I

The preparation

"A sharpened sword, once used has to be sharpened again"

Ling Chi

The importance of dreaming

Dream life is more important than we might initially think. If we give attention to it, if we take care of it, we will make better use of a good part of our time on Earth, since we spend approximately one-third of it sleeping.

Let us see why dream life is important.

First, because by means of it, the subconscious is unblocked of all that was repressed during the day. While awake, we keep up a natural self-control regarding our actions, thoughts and feelings. Whatever the amount of this self-control, our reactions are always supervised, which also brings many advantages. However, below the level of waking consciousness various movements, ways of feeling, and latent forms of thinking remain repressed and retained, and the dream constitutes an opportunity for their liberation. In general, we are freer in dreams. This is precisely because we do not exercise control over them, although it is possible in a more advanced stage of evolution to direct them to an intended outcome.

Here is an example of unblocking that occurred in the life of a soul. A student in parachute school dreamed that he lost control of his parachute and, unable to open it, he had a sensation of falling in the emptiness. Scared by this dream and taking it as a warning, he wanted to abandon the profession. However, he spoke about this to a specialist, who asked him if while he was awake, if he had ever passed through a similar experience during his parachute training. And he answered affirmatively. The student remembered one of his first jumps, when he couldn't open the parachute at first, but that the problem was resolved immediately, and he did not become scared. The specialist then explained to him that this dream occurred as a result of this incident and that, although he thought that it had not disturbed him when it happened, the fact remained as a piece of repressed shock, giving origin to the dream. This example also demonstrates how it is easy to take a different path from what the dream is indicating, through a wrong interpretation.

Dreams of falling however, do not always mean that an individual is going to fall and has repressed the fear in the subconscious, as in the case of this parachutist. Before sleep we can firmly hold the intention not only to register our dreams in the physical brain, but also to open ourselves to their comprehension. This is achieved with aspiration and with a sincere and pure will.

When we start to study dreams, it is good to take care in order to not acquire fixed ideas about their meanings. Consulting dictionaries of dreams or other guides of this nature will never bring you to an understanding of the issue since each dream is unique. Although two people may dream the same thing, the interpretation may be different for each one of them – therefore it is useless to limit yourself to pre-established meanings.

In my case, considering my temperament, a dream that I am falling or slipping is a message for me to be cautious because I might make a mistake soon after, maybe even on the same day. Dreams such as these are a warning that I have to be careful with my actions, feelings and thoughts – different from the case of the parachutist.

•••

We see, therefore, that it is not always useful to take the example of another for ourselves. This is why, in a book such as this one, the examples are given for us to become familiar with the topic, to open our minds, and to be familiar with other points of view.

•••

A second reason to value dreams is that they do not only unblock, as in the case of the parachutist, but also balance our conscious life. For example, people who live in polluted and unhealthy cities dream that they are in the country, in the fresh air, in beautiful places or in tranquil cities, leading a calm life. During a dream like this a balancing is taking place in the person, in their inner world, psychologically, and their subconscious is being enriched with the element of health.

Besides this, the actions in a dream may take place in a rhythm different from what we may observe when we are awake. And when this oneiric rhythm is more balanced, it also has the effect of harmonizing our busy external life.

•••

Another reason is that dreams may put us in contact with higher levels of our being, with the supra-conscious, from where there may come precise orientations for us, which in the waking state may not easily happen because of the distractions to which the brain and senses are exposed.

Van Gogh for example, would receive inspiration during dreams. While his physical body was sleeping, he would receive knowledge about what he must paint, registering what he had received and would execute when he was awake. Also Wagner, the musician, passed through this process. On one occasion, he heard in dream a part of an opera, which he then wrote down immediately upon waking.

•••

Still another reason to give value to dreams is that they may reveal that separation does not exist between human beings, and even between them and the universe. In the level of waking consciousness we have the illusion of being separate, one from another, i.e. from all humanity – to be one thing and the universe another thing as if it were distant and outside us. However, a dream can immediately show that this is not the reality.

Let us see as an example, a dream that demonstrates that there is no real separation between people and that it is impossible to isolate ourselves from the rest of humanity and from the events external to us. A ship was anchored in a port and thousands of people were trying to enter it, jostling each other with anxiety to be able to board the ship, with confusion around. The person who dreamed this was also one of the people in the dream and she was trying to enter onto the ship by passing in front of everyone. Then she heard an inner voice: "It is useless to do this because the ship will not leave until the last person has boarded; so instead of using so much force to try to pass in front of the others, it would be better if you move to be in the last place and help the others to board first."

When passing through a dream experience of this nature, an individual is marked positively and upon waking, perceives that something was transformed inside of themselves. All those who have had dreams like this one, which leave a strong mark, know that after this experience they cannot continue to be the same as before.

•••

The message that we must receive is not always contained completely within one dream. At times we have a series of them, as chapters of a book or of a story, and the indications are given to us little by little, in parts. Although on the surface these dreams do not reveal many links between them, in general they form a thread. This is why, when we have many dreams in one night, on following nights, or even with intervals between them, it is interesting to take note of them with as much faithfulness as possible and to date them. And after a certain amount of time to verify and accompany them, as if we were reading a book. Sometimes part of the indication is in some of the dreams and the conclusion in another, although at first look there seems to be a disconnection between the parts.

With regard to dreams in sequence, I knew someone who was studying a family problem, but his emotional involvement with his relatives did not allow him to see the situation with the necessary clarity. He made an internal request to dream about it and when he slept encountered his grandfather in astral plane, who told him with great sincerity and frankness, opposite to what was usually the case, letting him know the true situation of the family. Days after, when the person asked for confirmation regarding the words of the grandfather, he had another dream; in this one the family was traveling in a car and at a certain moment they arrived at the edge of a cliff. He jumped from the car in time not to go over the precipice with everyone else.

Therefore a dream may present points of view that actually come from our inner deeper side, and not from our more superficial, apparently rational, moral, religious or philosophic side; i.e., from our external structure. In some dreams, as we saw, these structures may be liberated, and then we find ourselves before the reality, seeing it with more clarity.

•••

Once we were in a group in another country, awaiting the visit of a couple who were coming from Brazil. Because they were so well known in Brazil, the members of the group were impacted by their coming, not knowing how to receive them or what to offer them. Then I asked myself before going to sleep what was the best way to relate with these visitors. There must be a correct form for this – I thought. What is being prepared to receive them evidently was artificial.

On the following morning, when I was about to open my eyes, I dreamed with two figures that symbolized the couple. On this level, in which nothing is masked, they were as small children. I did not know how old they were, because in dream the relation between size and age for children is not the same as in the physical plane – in this case they were as newborns walking. This is how they were, in the reality of the subtle level, these very well-known and important people who were going to arrive: they were delicate beings, small, and inexperienced, who must be treated in an appropriate way by all of us. This is what we did, and everything went well.

The more that we enter deeply into this issue, the more we will have symbolic dreams, linked to non-concrete facts. In many cases these dreams may be considered as a language of the soul.

When the soul speaks with us by means of a dream, it does not use normal language. Therefore, what comes to us is not rationally understandable, because it comes from an abstract non-logical plane. We see this in the dream just mentioned above, in which two adults who were considered to be mature in normal life appear in the symbolic plane as newborns. When considering a dream as this, it could be judged as nonsense. This language does not therefore obey logic and it cannot be understood only with the rational mind.

We cannot reach the soul with the common mind. In the waking life, one plus one is two, while in language of the soul it is not the same. If we interpret a symbolic dream in a rational way, it will be difficult to arrive at a correct conclusion.

The intellectual formulation, although it may be beneficial in some cases, may distort in other cases the perception and the comprehension of the true meaning of a symbol that is presented to us. We must then be careful not to face a symbol through the light of our own projections or theories, because the intellect belongs to the level of the concrete mind and the symbol may originate from a deeper level. It is a concentration of energy, a synthetic knowledge that we receive all at once without need to rationalize or deduce. When we interpret a symbol intellectually we distort the meaning.

With regard to symbols, there are some who dream of doors. At times these are shut, at other times they are opening. We could also dream that we are before an opened door. And so, as with every symbol, a door may have different meanings depending on the case. The human mind will find as many meanings as it has ideas, and it is probable that none of them will be real. This confirms the uselessness of searching for the meaning of dreams in books.

In a dream, a closed door may deliver many different messages, depending on the situation. It could be a suggestion to the person to not insist on something, because this direction is closed; or on the contrary, it may be suggesting that the person should place their hand on the door handle and open it, or even that it is meant for the person to find the key. In each of these cases there is a specific work to be done. We can also say that it is necessary to be patient in the face of an impasse, waiting for the moment of a new opportunity. We thus can see how many meanings a symbol is capable of presenting.

In order to know what the dream is manifesting it is necessary to denude ourselves of any preoccupation to see things with logic, to want to impose our ideas on its meaning. We have then, to liberate ourselves from concepts, otherwise we would not have the conditions to comprehend the symbol.

When recounting a dream, often this may result in the dreamer making comments about it, such as "This dream is important for me because it gives me understanding about many things" and so on and so forth. In this case because of the interference of the personality, the description becomes inauthentic, because it is polluted with the thought forms of the dreamer who has commented on their own dream. They emphasize certain parts more than others, they think that one part is more relevant than the other – bringing to the description an energy foreign to the dream, an energy that may influence the interpretation of its meaning.

In looking at a dream it is better to remain impartial, both when we share it with someone else – in which case this person may interpret it – or if we try to search for ourselves for its meaning.

It is good to register the dream with fidelity, without adding to it anything. We can say: "one door was closed" – and nothing more than this, except when there is some detail emphasized or to be observed in a particular way. The details of a dream are always important and revelatory. If I have dreamed with "a closed door" I must remain quiet and impartial to see if there comes to my mind other details. This is because a closed door may have a world of interpretations, but because I am not trained, I may end up seeing only the concrete image. However, if I connect myself in silence with the symbol that

I have seen, and if I remain very quiet, avoiding personal opinions, then it is likely that many other elements will begin to appear in my consciousness. I may then remember, for example, that "the door was white" or that "the handle was on the left side" and so on. These details can have a specific meaning, which will emerge from within me, not by means of mental explanations, but from transforming states of feeling.

But even if I am very quiet before the symbol, with an impartial attitude, I may not come to any conclusion. However, this does not matter; due to the simple fact that I have remained tranquil, impartial and impersonal, I allow the symbol to transform me. Due to it being a concentration of energy from another level, with my impartiality, even without understanding it, I end up entering into contact with the impulse that it brings.

•••

When we say that we understand a symbol, in reality we capture only one of its multiple aspects. A symbol has implications that we cannot reach. And if it is too abstract, in such a way that my current degree of understanding does not allow me to reach it, I only have to be relaxed to be touched by its energy.

If there was presented to me a vision of a star of five points, or one of six points, or a pitcher or a stick, without my capturing its meaning, I must not give importance to the fact that I do not know how to interpret it. If a symbol comes to me and I do not understand it, it is a signal that it came to me for me to simply remain before it and nothing more. It would not be constructive in these cases, for another person to try to interpret the symbol, since I may become conditioned to their point of view and it could be that their interpretation does not correspond to the fact that the symbol is trying to show to me. Perhaps the symbol wants to say nothing more than this: "stay calm, quiet and attentive, looking at me."

•••

In this undertaking we need to free ourselves from complexes of inferiority or superiority, or of self-sufficiency. This is because the latter may lead us to think that we can comprehend all dreams easily and the former because they may lead us to believe that we cannot approach this world of dreams, because up to this point no one has taught us to interpret them. We have to be free of all of this, because it is enough to remain before the symbol even without knowing what the meaning is, in order to receive the energy of the soul. The more abstract and incomprehensible is the seen or dreamed symbol, the deeper is the level from which it comes. Each time that we remember and we think of it, with gratitude and affection, we are energized and we connect with its origin. Our essence is being represented by the symbol, and because of this we are placed in contact with it every time the mind comes back to its representation, and in the proportion that this can be done in the present phase of our terrestrial evolution.

Deep sleep and other types of dreams

Not everyone has the inclination to remember their dreams. When we do not have this inclination, we should not force the recollection, because if we insist this can lead to fatigue of the brain cells and insomnia.

It is essential to be calm about this so that we do not disturb the deeper state of sleep which is extremely necessary. Dreams occur at first in the period that takes place from the time of the physical body becoming asleep until reaching the state of deep sleep. The latter therefore does not have dreams and its duration is only a few minutes. Through it we replenish the energy that we find in the intimacy of our being, an energy essential for the continuation of life.

During the time of returning from deep sleep to the consciousness of waking, dreams begin again. If during the day we are able to cultivate an attitude of non-harm, of non-criticism, of non-judgment, of absence of expectations, and without ambition, we will see that our sleep will be good and that deep sleep will really be restorative.

•••

In general, there are three ways in which we are trapped in illusion: the mental illusion of time and space, the consciousness of being a personal ego, and the conditioned behavior about sexuality. These limitations, of which we are not free either during the life of waking or during dream life, do not exist in deep sleep.

When we are immersed in deep sleep we lose the notion of time and space – which allows us to receive the necessary energy for the restoration of the mind. In the moment that we lose the consciousness of the personal being, we create the conditions for the rejuvenation of the physical cells and, thus we wake up with the forces restored. In the same way, the loss of consciousness of one's own sexuality in deep sleep brings about the regeneration of all of the energy system.

If we do not have a total, deep sleep, for at least a few minutes during each twenty-four hours, the circulatory and digestive systems will show signs of failure – which, with respect to the mind, prevents us from seeing things with clarity.

Both religiosity (i.e., the link between the levels of the personality and the super-conscious) and also the energy that impels us to philosophy, come from deep sleep. It is not the studies nor the experience of life that bring us to them; what impels us over time to search for reality by means of them is this brief contact with the depths of the being, repeated contact throughout all our existence during sleep.

•••

While the physical body is sleeping and the consciousness is gradually retracted from the bodies, dreams come in which the consciousness has experience of higher levels of experience, or in bodies beyond the physical, the emotional, and the mental. But, there is no reason to be dissatisfied if these experiences do not remain registered in the brain. Having faith, we perceive that what is registered is what is useful for the evolution of the external consciousness of the being in that moment. However, with a certain training and love for this process, and with time, we can acquire the capacity to register the dream, if appropriate.

•••

We call common and normal dreams those which are produced by the life of the desires. Desire is the secretion of the emotional body and because of this it defines some of the categories of common dreams for the great majority of people. However, over the course of this study we will give primary consideration to other kinds of dreams, those which are messages, expressions or precise orientations of the higher self, of transpersonal levels, i.e. levels beyond the personality.

In order to understand dreams of this second type, which in many cases are manifestations of the soul of the individual, we need something beyond analysis, deduction, or the experience of life. We need intuitive knowledge. As long as we do not acquire this knowledge, it is prudent to not interfere in the process of self-discovery of others with interpretation of their dreams. This is especially true if these require such an intuitive ability in order for them to be understood.

Let us now see this life of desires, which gives birth to ordinary, normal dreams.

To give an illustration, we can refer to the case of a person who had a sincere desire to be in peace and harmony with her own family, as well as to understand what she was living. She then dreamed that her two brothers and her mother were inside a type of "dome", while the father remained outside at a certain distance. Regarding the person who was dreaming, she was not participating in the scene but remained apart, only observing. Her positive desire brought to her this clarifying dream: her two brothers and her mother were living a process; the father another, and she did not have anything to do with that directly. Thus the dream revealed to her what she needed to know.

•••

Older desires, nourished in past lives, can also be manifested in dreams outside the context of the current life. I will next relate one of these dreams.

•••

A few years ago I was living with a very evolved person, with whom I had an emotional involvement in a past life. I did not know about that involvement from the past, being only conscious of our relations in the current phase, which were pure and elevated. However, one day without ever expecting or thinking about that, I dreamed that I was in an environment of previous centuries, in a certain part of Europe. I could recognize the place because in this lifetime I had visited that city, where in fact I always felt as if I were at home. In that dream I lived a series of experiences in different parts of the city, even feeling emotions that I must have had in the past. It was as if I were someone else, with those emotions that in the current life already had become retrograde for me. They were the desires and the feelings of a past incarnation that produced that dream.

•••

Another level of the life of desires that can give rise to common dreams is the astral or the collective-emotional. Considering that humanity as a whole has one emotional life, which is the astral, then it can in some way reach us insofar as we are members of it. I mention as an example the dream of a person who went to visit a coastal city, which seemed to be very geologically ancient, although its past was not well known. On opening the window of the hotel where she was staying, instead of seeing the city as it is today, she saw an ancient scene, with animals from that period of time as if it were a present reality. On commenting to us about what happened, it was clear to us that such a picture was created by the desire of many people who study and research this topic and who live in search of archeological data. Such desires created a scene in the astral plane, and this scene could be captured by someone else. With this we can see that we can have dreams not only when the physical body is sleeping, but also with open eyes, as in this case.

•••

Another kind of desire, very positive, that leads us to have dreams and is interesting for our own study is the desire to free ourselves from our limitations.

A woman was in conflict with her professional environment. Although that was a problem of her personality, already made conscious, she was at the point of no longer being able to stay there. Her desire to free herself from that environment produced the following dream: she was in the place of her work, in the midst of the usual irritations, and her attention was concentrated on three drawers of her desk, which in the dream appeared in view. Because in dreams space functions in another manner and we can see through an object, she saw that there was disorder inside the drawers. This was intended to tell her the following: "the disorder is inside yourself, in the physical level, in the emotional, and in the mental." Then all of a sudden the second drawer opened up, and insofar as each drawer represented one of these levels, it was the case that the second one represented the emotional. "Start by harmonizing the emotional level, this is more urgent," said the dream.

Evidently the solution was not to leave the job and arrange for another one, but to place the three bodies of the personality in order and in harmony.

•••

We must be equally thankful for any dream or experience that we have. A dream has value, whether it comes from the soul level or from the levels of the personality. In studying it, we order the themes in the mind and if we are grateful, we use them as instruments of transformation.

•••

Dreams generated by the life of desires can be useful to show us how much we still are circumscribed by the human levels. The understanding of the essence of the work with dreams can then bring us to free ourselves from the desires and to dispose us to higher aspirations and to the fulfillment of the will of the soul.

•••

There are methods that make it possible for us to be conscious of dream life, and three of them are commonly used. The first is self-analysis in which we try to re-live the past. This is not utilized in contemporary spiritual work because when we unravel the past, reconstruct and revive older situations, in the end we give to them more force.

In spiritual psychology the second and third methods are used, together or separately depending on the case. The second consists in making a creative life possible for the individual, in which one abandons the past and stops acting only for oneself as one has been doing, and begins to dedicate oneself to an altruistic activity. This form of work in the external life reflects itself in dreams, permitting the subjective world to flourish with superior quality, and by means of this the desires disappear little by little and the greater will emerges. This method of changing the life must be used to the extent that the individual can support it without excessive tensions.

The third method, according to esoteric psychology, consists in helping the individual to remember that she or he is a soul, a spiritual being. With positive thoughts we invoke the soul energies, both in the waking life and in the dream one. By constantly thinking of the soul and having it present in the consciousness, promising developments are triggered.

•••

As has already been said, many times dreams occur that are a continuation of previous dreams. This helps us to recognize that life is never interrupted as we sometimes think. By the way, I remember an experience of a person who dreamed something of great relevance for her evolution. She saw herself in a train station ready to make a long trip. It was clear that it concerned an inner voyage, which was symbolized by some familiar elements. However, in order to be attentive to what would pass in this important dream, she woke up and became conscious of the situation, assisted by the magical atmosphere of the train station. As a result of her awakening the experience permeated all the levels of the personality, arriving very clearly to the physical brain. She then took some notes from the beginning of the dream and returned to sleep. The dream continued almost immediately: she boarded the train and she received all the signals given by the conductor of the train that the trip was a form of preparation for a new phase of her life. This second part of the dream was rich: each detail that she perceived helped her to see things relating to her own development, preparing her for tests that came soon after in her waking life.

•••

The associations that the mind makes are not always useful for the comprehension of dreams. Mental freedom and availability are necessary in order to face each dream as if it were the first in life, as a process of self-discovery that begins in that moment, and in order to not allow the entrance of any preconceived beliefs created by the personality.

•••

The anxiety that some have when waking after a dream can prevent them from dreaming again for some time. As a result, this is the first obstacle that one may have to overcome. When we have a greater goal, such as for consciousness to penetrate the life of dream, the anxiety is generally resolved.

It is good for the mind to perceive the block that anxiety or expectation can create: when this is noted the mind can participate in the process of self-discovery more decidedly and positively, help the personality to free itself from these dregs.

Still, it can be pointed out that it is not always possible to free ourselves quickly from anxiety, although this can happen with individuals who have unshakeable faith and who surrender themselves entirely to the higher levels. Generally, it is more common that the anxiety dissolves itself slowly by means of loving, continuous and patient effort. When, in the course of the falls and the returns during tests, the mind is kept firm in the evolutionary goal, the anxiety is depleted. It may happen also that the energy of certain dreams dissolves this hindrance, allowing the individual to feel free from it when they wake up.

Falling asleep correctly

When we lie down and we prepare ourselves to sleep, the higher self begins to gather all the available energies, bringing them to the region of the cardiac center. It is important to accompany this movement towards the deeper levels, interiorizing ourselves and preparing for a tranquil sleep. Along with this introspective movement the thoughts that pass must be discarded or transformed into something better. In the same way, while the physical body rests, that which is still tumultuous in the emotional body must be appeased.

When the physical body and the brain sleep the soul retreats into its own level, which is the abstract mental or intuitive plane. From there the soul may or may not send impressions to the bodies of the personality. If the bodies are ready and resting, the messages of the soul can pass through them and be transmitted from the mental to the emotional, from the emotional to the etheric, and from the etheric to the physical brain. In this way when the body awakens after sleep, it will have registered in the brain what the soul has sent. However, if the body does not have the necessary relaxation, the message may not be able to overcome the barriers of the concrete mental, the nearest level to the region of the soul.

If the body does not have this relaxation, the physical brain will continue registering what is happening around it, as for example, the noises in the environment. With this, it will be prevented from capturing that which occurs in the subtle levels during the night, and when it captures it, it will do so imprecisely.

•••

If in the process of relaxation, we perceive that the preoccupations of the day are still accompanying us, we can use the resource of recapitulating it in reverse. Such a revision must be done in a calm, attentive and impartial manner in order to not provoke new involvements with facts already lived. The practical effect of this work is that the episodes of the day will be unrolled in the brain, as scenes of a movie, and end up being freed. The cerebral mechanism will remain free of these memories which would otherwise have the power to excite it during the night and cause it to continue functioning, producing the so-called cerebral dreams that do not have any evolutionary value.

Some individuals fall asleep during this recapitulation, which is not of concern, because what is important is the intention to complete it. This good intention is projected into the sleep state and the recapitulation can proceed when the person is already sleeping. This is not always conscious but it could be. I know of people who, when falling asleep in the middle of this work, have dreams that they are continuing it, and in fact this work is done in the astral plane – which is of equal value.

All of this is useful to demonstrate how much resonance there is in the subjective planes to our final intention before falling asleep.

•••

It is also necessary that the emotional body be in a state of relaxation, because the etheric counterpart of the brain is in contact with it, receiving both the positive currents as well as the negative ones. If the emotional is agitated, working on its own, the etheric brain will also do the same, even if the physical body is already asleep.

When we do not relax our emotional body before beginning sleep, it remains in contact with the emotional bodies of others linked with us. Then it collects feelings, impressions and sensations that were experienced during the day. Due to its capacity to dramatize, it creates a whole history with the material gathered, a history that the brain registers and presents as if it were an authentic dream.

We can relax the emotional body in the moment in which we look for a good position for sleep – one in which the physical body feels more comfortable and free – and in which we free the brain from the events of the day, by the backwards recapitulation. At this point, the emotional body must be wanting for the physical body and the brain to be asleep, in order for it by itself, to be ready to serve as a transmitter of the messages of the soul. At the time of the recapitulation, the emotional assumes the task of dis-identification from all that happened during the day, seeking for a calm and instructive night.

•••

The thinking mind, or the concrete mind, also may produce dreams on its own, because what happens during the day, or more so during everyday life, remains impressed on it. Beyond this, during sleep the mental body can make external contacts more easily than if the physical were awake. This occurs because the mental remains more free to go wherever it wants and make its movements; then entering into contact with other mental bodies of people who may or may not be sleeping, and bringing to itself the material that is circulating there. It sends the material to the brain, which presents it as if it were the individual's own dream.

The mental body allows us to act with the energy of will, which is not found in the other bodies of the personality. In this case it is enough to want to not suffer the influences of external thoughts, individual or collective. Thus, before going to sleep, we can say the following: "I do not want the mental to register what is going on outside of myself, nor that it makes contact with who I was with during the day, because I do not want to dream what these people are dreaming, nor to have their thoughts impressed on my brain." With the will focused in this way, but without rigidity or tension, the mental consciousness will answer in the desired way, assisted by the higher self.

Thus we have seen some of the steps that prepare the bodies for sleep: the relaxation of the physical, the work with the brain recapitulating in reverse the events of the day, the desire of the emotional to have an instructive night, and the will of the mental to not suffer interferences. As the mental is a subtler body of the personality, when we work with it, it is as if we were constructing a field of protection around the other bodies that compose the personality. Thus we enter into sleep in the correct way, leaving the bodies organized and prepared for the oneiric life of the higher level.

•••

When awake, it is as if we are inside of an armor, or shells, which are the bodies of the personality. They protect the soul from gross vibrations, which is necessary in order for it to live incarnated and to act in the three dimensions. But although they function as a protection that allows the soul to be manifested, if these armors are not disciplined, they will become an obstacle for what comes from the soul.

This alignment of the bodies can be done during the day, when we are awake. Thus, it does not matter what is the activity, the physical will be relaxed, the emotional serene, and the mental lucid. On this attitude will depend also what will be registered at night, during sleep. If the alignment is incomplete, the nocturnal result can be a dramatization that comes from each plane. Also it can happen that during sleep, elements from only one level are registered, and that which could come from the soul does not arrive to the conscious world of the individual.

•••

When we are falling asleep, it could be good if soon we reached, with consciousness, more profound zones of our being. There is a technique that can be used not only to remind us what passed during the night, but also to rapidly traverse the intermediary levels. This consists of taking special care with the last moment that precedes the time of falling sleep, the moment in which we are neither awake nor asleep, in which we are entering into the oneiric state. In this moment the last thought of the consciousness must be positive, imbued with the will to go to a much higher, superior level: a thought that is an affirmation of the spiritual world. This defines a more mature dream life.

This procedure is equally valid for the hour in which we will disincarnate. We can train ourselves each night when we go to sleep, enabling ourselves to be able to do this exercise at the moment of dis-incarnation, but with even greater repercussions: because the last thought determines a series of conditions for the future life.

•••

Regarding the habit of reading before falling asleep, various observations can be made. All readings link us with the mental plane of the writer or with the level that inspired them. If we read a detective story before sleep, we may go to the lower astral; but if we read a philosophical book of higher quality, we may go to the superior mental. Thus also, if we sleep soon after watching a news report on the television, we may enter into the vibration of the psychic environment that was shown to us.

There are people who keep a book on the night table to be read a little bit each night before sleep. On the quality of this book will depend the quality of the dream life. Having a book with elevated content allows us to enter into sleep in a good condition of relaxation after only a few paragraphs of reading. Nonetheless, one has to have prudence, because if the book is extremely interesting or provokes excitement, it may absorb the individual so much that it leads them to read instead of to sleep.

∙∙∙

It is impossible to suggest to different people the same technique for sleeping correctly. Each individual is at a different evolutionary point and therefore they may have different needs. Furthermore, each one has their own path of least resistance in the execution of diverse activities, a path that varies according to their temperament and which needs to be discovered in order to be respected. There are people who without any effort, have lucid dreams as they have already done work in past lives. In this case it is enough for them when they are going to sleep, to concentrate for a few moments on the center of their own being and they will then go directly to the most elevated level that the consciousness is able to reach.

∙∙∙

Another point to be considered is the time of going to sleep. It is good to have a fixed, regular time. We may be reminded that the subconscious is full of rhythms, and if we establish one more rhythm voluntarily, it will be absorbed well.

The use of these techniques, or of others, must not be permanent. When self-control is achieved, the person discovers the discipline that suits them.

In the end everything is done in a natural and simple way, in one's own way; and one may also receive an inner orientation regarding this subject, something which usually occurs at a certain point.

Waking up correctly

Here we make a recommendation to those who have the intention to wake up correctly. There exists a moment of perception that is very short, an instant in which we perceive that we are waking and in which we recapitulate the events of the night. It is in this moment of perception that we need to have care in order to not allow preoccupations or plans for the new day to enter. Therefore, when we have consciousness that we are waking, we have to try in this moment to remain immobile and without thinking of anything.

Achieving this silence, we perceive the awakening of the body and we take care to not move it, especially the head. This care is necessary because when we move the physical body we may erase the memories of what we dreamed. A simple movement of the head can alter the whole reality of a dream.

If a dream has to come to memory, it may happen during this special moment; if we remember only one part of the dream, it is enough to have it present so that the other memories may come up little by little. If we remember initially only the end or the beginning of the dream, it is good to not force its complete re-composition, in this case it is enough to remember the dream in reverse until we have reconstructed it totally. Even to remember it in part can be useful.

There are cases in which after this tranquil awakening the dream comes to memory all at once and it is not necessary to recapitulate it. Even so, we must remain quiet with all the previously mentioned care; otherwise everything is erased and the dream that had been captured disappears also.

The entire dream does not always offer material for reflection. It may seem that we are provided with an intelligent mechanism that selects what is necessary to remember. It is as if the consciousness of the physical body in attunement with the higher self only brings to memory the part of the dream which has symbolic meaning and that brings lessons to us.

When the dream has come to memory, we may write it down before passing on to remembering another dream that may have occurred in the same night. We write slowly what we have been able to remember, without agitation and with the maximum possible gentleness and harmony. After writing down the basic points of a dream, or all of it, we return our attention to the second dream that is coming to memory, and so on.

If there is any doubt about the fidelity of what was written down, we may make the recapitulation two or three more times, in order for it to be more accurate. If perhaps we do not have success in our goal of remembering a dream, when wake up we must continue to be imbued with the same disposition, alert for the eventual reception of a message. It is enough to keep this intention in order to open the channel that will allow the memory of the dream, even in the midst of our normal daily tasks.

We may remember a dream that we had some time ago and this may happen when the correct moment arrives for it to be remembered. It may have happened that, when we recapitulate the dream, it may become vague or nebulous. However, a dream never is lost, it is never withdrawn from the consciousness – and it is enough for us to remain trusting and positive and we will be giving an opportunity for it to reappear.

•••

That which occurs during the night may not be immediately imprinted on the consciousness. Even during the day we might have experience of some activities in other levels which probably will only be registered in the moment of waking, i.e. after the brain has become rested and receptive. Then in the morning what happened in the subtle bodies during the day before, or even earlier, may emerge in the memory as if it were an experience occurring that night.

•••

After a creative night, we will be transformed, primarily if our deeper sleep was profitable. If the messages of our inner being do not remain only in the subconscious level or in the unconscious, but come to be known by the personality, it may cooperate in this transformation.

There are some who have great ideas when they awake. In order for those who have these tendencies to develop them in a healthy way we recommend that, before sleep, they see with clarity the issue to be resolved and that they surrender it to the super-consciousness. Sending it to depths of the being and no longer thinking about it, the solution may imprint itself in the physical brain at the moment of waking.

To a lesser degree, during the time of a nap we could also do this same work and the result will also be to obtain clear answers.

•••

In the event that sleep is interrupted by the movement of someone near or by an alarm clock, the consciousness has to quickly go back inside of the body. Such an interruption could eliminate the possibility for the person to remember what has passed during sleep, or to be able to do the recapitulation in an orderly way. Those who use alarm clocks ignore the fact that the physical body has its own consciousness, capable of attending to the requests that are made to it. For us to awaken at the time that we need is one of the more common services that the consciousness of the physical body can provide. As this ability is always active it is enough to ask it to awaken the physical body at a determined time and it will comply.

If we have to wake up someone else, we must do it in the gentlest way possible, and not brusquely.

Even if we adopt all of these positive attitudes, it is good to remember that the unfolding of events in the inner levels during the sleep of the physical body are outside of our control – except in the case of the common normal dream, produced by desire, which can even be directed if we are well-trained.

The adventure of the night

We have to create within ourselves an appropriate state so that revelation through dreams will be possible. One of the basic strategies for this is for us to consider the life during sleep and the life of dream as a continuation of the waking state and vice-versa.

I remember here the story of a writer who, when he reviewed the book that he had just finished writing, thought that he needed to make some alterations in a specific chapter. He felt that something was not correct but did not have consciousness of what it was. As his friends who read the book could not identify the error, he resolved to resort to his dream life. He then dreamed of some armchairs. As soon as he noticed them he saw that they began to reverse their positions and he strongly impressed in his mind the place that each one was moving to.

When he woke up the next day, he knew intuitively that there in the dream was the solution for the chapter, and concentrating himself, he noticed that the number of paragraphs of the problematic page had the same number as there were armchairs in the dream. Then he identified the chairs with the order of the paragraphs and he cut them out and reversed their positions, reconstructing the change that had occurred with the armchairs.

In this way the problem that was presented in the waking life of this writer was solved in dream and was resolved on the next day when he, in the physical plane, placed the paragraphs in the order that was shown to him.

To consider our life on Earth while incarnated – as well as our life in other dimensions, when disincarnated, and also the states of waking and dream – as mere facets of the one and only existence is more intelligent and facilitates the contact with the superior worlds.

•••

Every night we live a process similar to what is inappropriately called "death." The difference is that in sleep the thread of life does not disconnect from the heart, whereas what passes at the end of an incarnation is that this thread is broken, separating itself also from the brain. In both cases, i.e. when disincarnated and when asleep, if we keep ourselves limited to the astral or emotional plane, we may encounter friends and others who we know, and re-create environments where we lived in the physical plane. If we keep ourselves limited to the inferior mental plane, we could restrict ourselves to the conditioning of the terrestrial life. There are however, fuller experiences awaiting us in the freedom of the higher levels of consciousness. We can begin to prepare ourselves for the great adventure that is called "death" by remaining conscious of what passes during dream.

•••

The study of dreams occurring during the early hours of the night generally is of little interest. Normally these dreams are reflections of what took place during the day. With a heavy blanket or excessive wool clothing, in the early stage of sleep for example, we could have the sensations that we are being pursued by a ferocious animal. There is also the case of those who enter into this phase with their brain still connected to external things, so that the ticking of a nearby clock is turned into a marching army battalion.

On the other hand, somnambulism is caused by the strong attraction which the physical body feels in relationship to the other subtle bodies of the individual. Due to this attraction, the physical body follows them when they detach during sleep. This is because the field of action of the physical body is limited to walk only in its surroundings, without being able to accompany the other bodies in their travels in the subtle worlds.

We must not awaken a somnambulist abruptly, because could they experience this as a sudden consciousness of a danger in the physical plane and with this lose their equilibrium or have a nervous shock. After naturally awakening however, someone may be made conscious about their somnambulism. If before falling asleep the person gives a decisive and clear mental order to the physical body so that it does not rise up and follow the other bodies, the somnambulism may cease.

•••

Regarding insomnia, we may say in general that it is caused by fear of the revelations that a dream can bring. We have insomnia from not wanting to enter into contact with the unknown nucleus of our being, from not wanting to know how we really behave, from not wanting to receive messages which could take us from our routine. It is a childish defense of the personality.

If someone is born with a tendency for insomnia, it is because in a previous incarnation they did not want to know the truth about themselves, however much it tried to reveal itself. The solution for insomnia is to decide to accept the truth without any fear.

A sporadic insomnia however, may not be due to this kind of fear. It is possible to resolve it in a simple way: it is enough for us to not force sleep and instead to try to do something practical and useful. I knew a person who put their closet in order when unable to sleep.

Sedatives or medicines for sleep may aggravate the situation because they numb the cerebral mechanism. If the inner problem of not deciding to know the truth about oneself is not resolved, the sedative is of no use. Sleep induced by sedatives is merely a coarsening of the brain.

•••

To talk during sleep may be explained as a refusal of the mental body of the individual to let the brain sleep. The mind continues its link with the happenings of the day and we speak, transmitting a part of what it is elaborating. This occurrence may be avoided by giving a precise order to the mental body before sleep, such as: "you may not continue working mechanically." It customarily obeys if the order is decisive.

Children who speak while sleeping also do so because of the movement of the brain, which remains involved with what happened during the day. Because the child may not have the ability to proceed in the same way as proposed above, it will be better to not interfere and wait for this phase of speaking at night to pass over naturally.

We may observe that during the full moon we speak more during sleep. This occurs because the forces of the moon exert a very strong influence upon the animal nature of the human being and may stimulate their physical cerebral side, as well as the astral.

•••

Let us focus now on the duration and rhythms of sleep. What is normal is that after falling asleep we spend some time entering into the world of dreams, passing two or three hours there in what is an intermediary phase, and after we enter into deep sleep. Soon after we pass again for a few hours into the intermediary phase and we spend some more time coming back to the physical cerebral consciousness. We see with this that at least seven hours are necessary in order to correctly experience all of this process. The majority of people need eight hours and others a little less. However, for the process to take place in an orderly fashion but in less than seven hours, it is necessary to have the attention be especially polarized in the deeper levels of the being while in the waking state and not only in the hours of sleep. If during the day we normally are linked to this deeper level, we will sleep less without prejudicing our health. However, this must be done in a spontaneous, unprovoked way.

•••

The quality of sleep depends on whether or not we are very oriented towards the physical material life, and on the degree of our detachment from everything that refers to it. It also depends on how much we are linked to the emotions. According to our degree of involvement, we pass more or less time in the astral plane, which is as illusory as the physical, in comparison with the consciousness of other dimensions.

It should be emphasized that the goal of those who search for a fuller life is to penetrate deeper levels, although, as we have seen, the fact that they spend a short period of time in the intermediate planes serves to liberate repressions. While the consciousness plunges into the depths, the bodies of the personality contact healing energies in the emotional plane or in the collective mental plane and after awakening they are restored.

It is common for people to say that they do not have time to sleep seven or eight hours daily due to their having more serious things to do. They do not perceive that sleep is a part of their existence that is just as important as the hours of waking, because through it we enter into contact with more elevated vibrations, changing for better the tone of our lives, with many beneficial consequences.

•••

Superficial conversations and depressing readings during the day lead us at night to a corresponding level of vibration.

•••

A refusal, even when unconscious, in wanting to know the truth about ourselves could impede us from having consciousness of the oneiric life, in which we see ourselves exactly as we are.

•••

Another fact that could interfere in the quality and the rhythm of the sleep is the situation when the person wakes up many times during the night. There are cases when this is frequent. It is possible that we do not achieve a continuous and healthy sleep because of the agitation during the day. However, it could also happen that we wake up many times during the night because nature and the higher self are using this situation to help us to remember what is passing in each phase of sleep and to appreciate this experience.

•••

Regarding those who have external activities during the night and who then sleep during the day, if they are doing this for karmic reasons and with inner consent they will not become physically exhausted, because in this case the organism and the body will adapt. But on the contrary, if this rhythm of activities is assumed for personal reasons, with time it will provoke an unbalance of health.

•••

In order to help people to go deeper into sleep more easily, we will make some observations about the rhythm of the night. It is not our intention to impose rules of behavior but only to give some fundamental information about the cosmic rhythm, in this way facilitating decisions.

Dusk represents a moment of general relaxation and this is a good time for us to begin to surrender to the necessary releasing. Until 10:30 p.m., it is still not fully night, but it is an intermediate period. From this time until 2:30 a.m. we are in the deepest part of the night. In contrast to the daily hours, in it are present energies that conduct us to a greater in-gathering. The energies of the day, with the light of the sun, lead us to the outside for external activities and to lucid action. Regarding the energies of the night, they conduct us into inner activity, to the reunion of the forces in the center of one's own consciousness. Considering this, if it were possible for us to be asleep between 10:30 p.m. and 2:30 a.m. in the middle of the night, we would be more harmonized with the energetic circumstances of this period, which facilitates not only deeper sleep but also the correct experience of all phases of sleep.

A lack of concentration in the waking life is caused almost always by a night of bad, disorganized sleep in which we do not accompany the basic cosmic rhythm.

It is possible that even if we do not observe these normal elements, we may remember our dreams well. Some sleep even when tired and unprepared, and nonetheless they have clear dreams. However, these constitute exceptions. These are sporadic cases in which the higher self manages to supplant the barriers formed by the habits of the personality and be present with its unlimited power.

Some cautions

To be kind with others is one of the key points for us to be able to become conscious of dreams. In contrast, the critical spirit carries the mind's tensions which tightens the brain, affecting its sensibility. In the same way simplicity of the heart is necessary, which emerges when we focus our consciousness for long times on the soul, remembering it frequently. With the practice of having it always in the mind we transform ourselves into simple people who are less proud and vain.

•••

Generosity is another important quality to be developed in order for the life of dreams to become useful. It links us with more elevated levels of existence and dissolves egocentrism, one of the greatest obstacles to the clarity of vision needed for dreams. Egocentrics who think only of themselves distance themselves from the higher world, which, although present within them, is not perceived.

•••

The fact of having good energy, of being well vitalized during the day, is good for the process of inner discovery through the oneiric life. Devitalization brings inertia, leaving the brain lethargic. If such energetic states are occasioned by the way that we live, then creating order in our everyday life is a priority.

•••

People who act from self-interest, with excessive preoccupation to obtain results, stay linked to the terrestrial vibrations and remain at this level while sleeping, creating difficulties for being conscious of dream life. This is not to say that we must not be practical, because practicality is a necessary condition for us to face physical life properly. What has to be avoided is to act looking for something in return. In dream, this "practicality" is useless because in the subtle dimensions, it is not necessary to fight for what we need – everything comes to us as if by magic, if it really has to come.

It is said that once Mozart had a piece of music to compose, and going around the city by carriage, he slept sitting on the carriage bench. Although the carriage was bouncing a lot, even so, he was able to sleep. Then he dreamed the piece that he needed to compose, hearing it in its entirety. When the carriage arrived to its destination he woke up and could write it down.

Considering this illustrative fact, we remain with the question: is it necessary for us to be so utilitarian?

•••

Whoever has difficulty with sleep can create by the force of thought a protective cover in the subtle matter of other levels and thus push away external influences during sleep. This covering, constructed with the imagination, prevents these influences from penetrating the aura of one's own being.

•••

When we become spectators of our own selves, we become able to take certain actions in the middle of a nightmare and even invoke a superior force. This, when done on the astral plane (the level where nightmares occur), dissolves everything immediately.

•••

A nightmare also can be dissolved by means of the practice of making in dreams the well-known sign of the cross. This universal symbol is as ancient as the Earth itself and is imprinted in all levels of consciousness. Besides this, it carries the positive energy of the millions of devotees who have had the cross throughout all time. Even when, in nightmares, we feel our limbs paralyzed, which is a common happening because of the vibration of the lower astral, we can make the sign of the cross mentally while we are sleeping, which has a much more rapid effect.

If before sleeping, we make the decision to make this sign during sleep, surely we will remember it and we will make it when it is necessary.

Nonetheless, the work that eliminates for good the tendency to have nightmares is that which we do with our own character. When we eliminate from the life of waking the tendencies of possessiveness, aggressiveness and egoism, nightmares will no longer present themselves. These tendencies serve as open doors for the astral forces that produce this type of dream.

•••

It may also happen that during the night a person could feel possessed by strange entities, that remain on the Earth. If this occurs with frequency it is a sign that reasons of a personal intimate nature linked to the person are allowing this. For example, certain negative traces in the character, such as ambition and insincerity, which may come from other incarnations, when they continue to be cultivated by the individual can produce an opening for these entities. Often these entities are artificial as they do not contain life in their nuclei. In other words, many "entities" which torment us in dreams are thought forms and not beings as we think.

Finally, a fundamental condition in order for dream life to be balanced and healthy is to have clarity about the importance of altruistic services, indispensable today because of the new energies that are penetrating planet Earth, especially those which come from the constellation of *Aquarius*. The One and Only Life is zealous for the evolution of its parts, and when we have decided to serve as a part of a group, or as individual members of humanity in general, we attune ourselves with the forces that sustain this life and bring us to continued progress.

Consequences of dreams

Dreams can also help us to approach three aspects of life which are considered complicated from the mental point of view, i.e. according to the limited perspective of the common consciousness.

The first is the fact of reincarnation. As an example, we can refer to well-known episode in which Zacharias dreamed of an angel. It said to him that his wife, Isabel, although sterile and aged, would have a child. It was revealed later also that this son would have the spirit and strength of Elijah, a prophet who had lived on Earth a long time before. Thus, Zacharias knew that his son would be the reincarnation of this prophet, something that was confirmed many times over the centuries by occultists.

In addition, a scientific research study titled "Twenty Cases Suggestive of Reincarnation," conducted in many countries, referred to a case that happened in Alaska. An older fisherman affirmed to his son that when he would reincarnate, he would come again as a member of the same family. Some days after the older man drowned in the ocean. A few months passed and the wife of the son, the daughter-in-law of the older fisherman, became pregnant and during the gestation period she dreamt that the father-in-law told her that he was being prepared to come back to Earth as her son. In fact, when the child was born, it showed on its physical body identical signs to those that were observed on the body of the older fisherman and they were located in the same places. While it was growing, the child evidenced more and more of temperament of the grandfather and the parents confirmed that the child was a living "picture" of him. This is explained by the fact that the period in which the fisherman was disincarnated was so short, that it rendered impossible the changing of the three bodies of the personality.

The second aspect is the existence of the soul. It is actually possible to dream with symbols about the soul, i.e. our higher self. There are people who dream, for example, of a bird and while asleep they recognize it as this higher self, through an inner certainty.

When we are awake we also have experiences that bring us to recognize the existence of the soul. There are those who have conscious contact with this inner nucleus, but the majority of people perceive it only in an indirect manner, through events in life, evidently directed by a greater force.

The third aspect of life that we can approach by means of dreams is the fact that we accomplish tasks while sleeping. With this, we change the idea that in sleep we disconnect from everything. In truth, there are people who, while asleep accomplish a certain type of work, using their subtle bodies moved by a higher consciousness.

A well-known occultist from the past revealed how her astral body, conducted by her soul, worked during physical sleep. She recounted that in the astral plane she went to a shipwreck, and that she was placed into service to rescue the people, and how one of the ship's masts fell on her shoulder. When she awoke she found that her physical body had a mark from this blow – providing concrete proof that the activity had been real.

The higher self can continue working in the night by means of the subtle vehicles while the physical is asleep. Little by little we can absorb this training, which progressing can bring us to the point of assuming tasks that are more and more useful. In this type of service, we primarily relate with individuals, helping them in some way; after with groups; and in a more advanced phase we pass on to planetary service.

I lived with a person who worked on this more advanced level and who, because of this, needed to be protected during the night. There was usually silence in the house and the person slept alone in her own bedroom. One morning she told me that during sleep, that she had participated in a meeting with well-known international politicians and that her task was to be present as a consciousness, radiating vital energy for the whole group. When the daily newspaper arrived we could confirm in news the success of an important meeting, the one in which this person had participated in her subtle body hours before.

•••

These works are regulated by the higher self of an individual, which has its own life on elevated levels of consciousness. For this, its astral and mental bodies can be dislocated at will for the execution of tasks. There already exist innumerable astral and mental bodies which loan themselves to this type of service, and the human consciousness of the individual does not always perceive this.

Personally I passed through this experience of being helped by someone else in such conditions during a particular difficulty. I was taking a spiritual retreat near Rome, in a place where there were many mosquitos. During the night the bedroom was full of them and I could not sleep. Because I was in a remote place where there was no access to repellants, and as the mosquitos were increasing, one night I closed my eyes and asked for help. I did this in order to be able to sleep – a goal that I accomplished afterwards. I slept and, finding myself lucid on the astral plane, I noticed that entering into my bedroom was a lady who I had never seen before, wearing a peasant's shawl that covered her head. She brought with her in her hand a plate full of charcoal with something burning – maybe some kind of incense. Thus, in the astral plane she entered into my bedroom, and showing to me something that was making smoke, disappeared leaving a scent of perfume. After that moment and until the retreat was concluded, I did not have any problem with mosquitos.

•••

The higher self also can work through its own body, technically called "causal" by esoteric psychology, or it can use any vehicle of the personality, as we have seen. If we become conscious of these dreams, or the work of other people on this level, it will help us to develop good will and altruistic services in the common human life.

•••

There are people to whom there is given the ability to serve more easily in the subtle levels than on the physical plane. What happens is that these levels do not present obstacles, whereas in the external level the interference of unfavorable karmic factors is possible. In general, in this type of work conducted in the subtle levels, a progression is observed. Thus, one who has the intention to serve humanity can be trained for this, which could happen also during the sleep of the physical vehicle.

I knew one of these servers of the world who had a common anonymous human life. Those who saw him did not perceive the existence of this intense nocturnal activity unless he revealed it, as he did with me. He told me that he had witnessed the suicide of a woman that took place in Spain. In "dream" he helped her higher self to retreat from the impure human vehicles. At a certain point in this activity, which was done with the radiation of the pure love of the soul, the figure of this person transformed into a historical Spanish personality, who in her time, had perpetuated slaughters. The following day after this report, the newspaper reported the suicide. It was with reference to a famous movie actress who the dream demonstrated had been the reincarnation of this historical personality. Thus, she passed through violence in a process of karmic equilibrium, as it is known by law that violence generates violence; i.e. by practicing violence towards others in the end we end up experiencing it profoundly in our own selves, with its consequences.

•••

The following episode which I will report next reveals the evolution of the consciousness of this server who, afterward began to accomplish a work with groups. Soon after he had helped the person who suicided, he reported to me that in dream he found himself in Vietnam collaborating with a group of soldiers in order for them to cross a bridge. In the dream the nationality of the soldiers was not specified. He told me "Six others and I were in a river holding up a bridge that was ready to collapse. At the same time, the soldiers passed over it and were able to reach the other shore." After this, we saw a bombing occur exactly over the area that the soldiers had just abandoned. In this way, all of them were saved. The following day the newspaper had news with respect to major bombings occurring in Vietnam and the escape of many groups of soldiers.

We may highlight some interesting aspects of this experience. The first is that of seven people who did not know each other on the physical plane and also, that they did not have any awareness of whether or not they were incarnated. Another interesting fact is that only seven people were able, in this other dimension of life, to hold up by themselves a bridge upon which were passing an entire troop of soldiers.

•••

There are various types of help that we may give and receive by means of activities undertaken in other dimensions. Once I had a problem with my physical eyes that eye doctors and regular medical doctors did not know how to explain. On my part I perceived that it was about something that needed to be resolved in another level of consciousness, that it was a disequilibrium which was reflected in the physical plane. For sure, it was regarding a block on a subtle level, possibly in the mental. I had the strong intention to dissolve it, not because of the eyes but for it itself. It was something to be resolved internally before the physical discomfort would disappear. When the desire to have a good eye was completely transformed into the idea of only resolving the main question, i.e. the cause of the illness, I had the impulse to purify myself.

Then something very significant happened: at night, after surrendering in the best way that I could, I slept and I had a dream. In it appeared a surgeon who operated on my eye using a scalpel whose touch I could feel on the eyeball without, however, suffering any pain. I accompanied the whole operation with lucidity, and when I woke up I went to the mirror to see if the work had left any mark. There were no external marks of the operation, but the eyes were completely good.

•••

Bad events in dreams may have positive results in human life if we have discernment about them. For example, a friend dreamed that she was being murdered by the man with whom she, in waking life, maintained an emotional involvement and a sexual relationship. The experience of suffering the murder in the dream left very deep marks in her so that it became impossible to continue with the relationship in the physical plane. The dream helped her to see what the quality was of her relationship, which, by the way, was killing her in certain ways. She told me that if it were not for the dream, she never would have had the strength to separate from the partner.

Common dreams and mental dreams

Here, in order to examine them more precisely, I resume the discussion of the two types of dreams already mentioned. It is good to accustom ourselves to observe all aspects of a dream because sometimes the key to its comprehension could be in a detail that normally would be unnoticed.

A Christian visionary, in her desire to serve Jesus, had a dream in which he appeared bringing a lamb in one arm. She interpreted it as approval for the work that she was doing – altruistic work of prayer and healing with individuals and groups – and she ended up becoming proud regarding the dream. Because the vision had been pleasant for her, she asked for it to be repeated, and the picture from the dream was again projected on her mental screen.

I transcribed in detail the dialogue which we had soon after she described to me the second dream, which to her seemed identical to the first.

- "But were they the same, the two pictures? You didn't see any detail that was different in the second from the first?" I asked her.

- "No" she answered me. "They were the same in every detail."

- "Then, repeat how was the first picture."

- "I saw Jesus, all in color, very beautiful, with a lamb in his arm."

- "In which arm?"

- "In the right."

- "Now describe the second" I asked her.

- "In the second, Jesus also was very beautiful as in the first, with a lamb in his arm."

- Then she made a pause, reflected a little, and completed: "only that in the second the lamb was in the left arm."

I could then call her attention to the importance of these details, since the lamb in the left arm was showing that the second image was constructed not by the authentic force that created the first, but by another that came to feed her human vanity. The second picture was not truthful, at least from the point of view of the evolution of the being.

If this simple detail had not been noticed, the visionary would have continued deluding herself and engaged in a path that she herself really did not want to pursue.

•••

Generally we do not give importance to details. In dream, however, some need to be noticed, as for example the side (right or left) in which an object or a creature is found. For the people who I knew and who reported to me their dreams and visions, the right side had positive value, whereas the left side had negative implications.

When I ask my inner world if I need to write a certain letter, I usually receive an answer with a vision of a sealed envelope. If the stamp is found on the right of the envelope, it means that I need to write the letter; but if it is on the left, that I must not do this. However, this must not become a pattern for all dreams, because as we saw, each one has their own world of symbols. Even when it is regarding a universal symbol, it is necessary to have caution in order that one has the correct comprehension of the message.

•••

Another type of common dream, with universal symbolism, refers to upcoming encounters that we have planned. If an encounter is positive, the person who we are going to see is presented on the right, or walking from the left to the right. On the contrary if it is unfavorable, the person goes towards the left, or shows up looking to the left, or some other clarifying detail manifests in the same direction.

•••

It is good to listen to the description of a dream with "two different ears." With one of them we listen attentively and lovingly to what the person is reporting, with the other – the inner ear – we listen to what the person actually is trying to say and to what in truth has occurred, independent of their projections about what has happened. This type of double antenna is necessary and must be used not only in relationship to others but, above all, with ourselves.

•••

If there is a collaboration among two people who study dreams, the key for the interpretation for the oneiric experience of one could manifest in the other. This could happen when there is an interaction of intentions or the same spiritual goal. Sometimes someone is not in the condition to receive the message because their channel for capturing the dream is not free enough, and then the message may be received by the partner.

I had an interesting experience in this regard. A friend told me that he had an analytic psychological treatment for eight years and had not received, up until then, an answer for a doubt that he had about himself. Evidently, he had in himself a block in a certain area, a block that became accentuated the more that he spoke about and concentrated on the issue. I suggested to him to consider these eight years as a stimulus for him to renovate his disposition for knowing the truth by using another process, less rational. I offered myself to help him search together for this truth and he accepted. I told him then that we must not speak any more about the problem and that, when we met again, that we would speak about other things. He agreed with this, and this opening soon provoked, on the very next day, each one of us to have a dream.

In his dream, he simply appeared standing in front of an elevator, and nothing more. It was only the elevator and him, facing the door. It may be observed that when he renounced his insistence on reflecting about the traits of his own personality, there came to him a symbol of ascension. After eight years of being in the dark, this little dream was a step. On my part, I also had made it possible to free myself from thinking about the issue, and on the same night I dreamed with him and the elevator; only that in my dream there was also a younger woman and he, facing the door, was making signs to her to enter it. A little later, in our normal conversation, each one recounted their dream and everything was becoming clear. In the dream that I had, he and the younger woman were side by side, which means that they were the same person: the active pole (the masculine) and the receiving pole (the feminine) of the same individual. The signs that he was making to the younger woman to come into the elevator were trying to say that he needed to let his feminine side to emerge, rise up, grow, surface and so on. We interpreted this as his affective and embracing side.

The desire to know the truth and the renunciation of any compulsion is what caused the truth to arise. In the current civilization, especially among some who are in a masculine body, there is still an inhibition in relationship to affective expressions. But it was enough for my friend to begin the inner work and free himself from this cultural conditioning (which we were working with in our conversations) so that in him there could come about the transformation. We found, in this way, that to work in conjunction can be useful when there exists an attunement between the two people.

•••

Other dreams in this same category are produced by a desire to meet people on the astral plane. They seem to be real and they reproduce the situations that we habitually live with these persons. They offer an opportunity to know about our tendencies, as on this higher plane we can act in an uninhibited way. And so, the energy expended in these meetings which are interesting only on the emotional level, can be more useful if they are expanded into another level, where the reality is transpersonal and the connections are true.

•••

Still, there are dreams that are a mere continuation or a reminiscence of our daily life, without any symbolic or evolutionary value. We may consider them in order to observe how we are acting – which allows us to make a revision in our attitudes when awake.

•••

Dreams of a mental nature, as I have already had occasion to mention, are more useful than astral or emotional dreams. In them, we are more in contact with ideas and ideals and not so much with emotions and human sentiments. These mental dreams imply a work of development of the mind by means of attunement with more far-reaching or altruistic conceptions.

An example of a mental dream with profound repercussions in the personality was the following: a younger man was searching to know the truth and asked for it to be revealed to him, whatever it might be. Because his request had sincerity it was responded to almost immediately by the higher levels of his mental plane. In this way, he dreamed with somebody who was coming out from inside of some filing cabinets and was opening a book in front of him, showing him an unknown alphabet. Although on the rational level the alphabet was totally unknown to him, the younger man had consciousness that it was real. In fact, when he awoke he felt that he had experienced a change because he was more secure and less curious, even though he did not understand the writing in the book.

In this dream, the one who presented the book was an aspect of himself, in this case an aspect that was familiar with a certain kind of knowledge. In this experience, he himself did not learn anything concrete, but his mind was able to register a lesson that had repercussions by non-rational means.

Each superior mind has its own method of establishing contact with the conscious self. As a result, when facing mental dreams we have to have patience because they are presented to us according to the type of energy manifested by our mind. When the message is incomprehensible to the normal mind, it means that the comprehension or the synthesis took place on another level – as is the case of the dream that came out from the filing cabinets.

• • •

I had the following experience in the realm of mental dreams: I was living through a cycle in which everything appeared to me to be very clear, without realizing how this had taken place. One day I laid down after lunch and soon after, passing through the cerebral and astral part of my being, in a few moments I found myself in a mental dream. In this level of consciousness, I could perceive a being dressed all in white, a whiteness that was merged with the background of the scene: it was as if there was one only color, or better, an absence of color. That being, a benefic figure had in his hand a pointer, a type of indicator that teachers use to point out the writing on the black-board. With this object he pointed to a church, much smaller than himself. It was a gothic church in miniature but clear in all details. When I fixed my attention on it, the dream ended.

A few days after when I was looking at the back cover of a book, I saw the picture of the author and I confirmed that it was the being who had shown up in my recent mental dream. The picture was of a well-known representative of the Catholic Church who had already disincarnated. I took the book, I opened it with attention, and I perceived that it contained teachings that amazingly, I had already received by other means. Relating the facts with the dream that I had, I perceived that the contents of the book had been completely transmitted to me at the moment in which the pointer indicated the miniature gothic church. The encounter with the book in the physical plane served to confirm for me the importance of mental dreams. From what I know, these types of dreams are possible when we disconnect enough from trivial preoccupations, commonplace desires, emotions and sensations, thus allowing the deeper levels to reveal themselves and to bring to us their synthetic teaching, without words.

•••

Geometric figures are also a part of the mental world and from them come much energy. Instead of receiving a response projected in the astral as if it were a movie with a plot, we could obtain it by means of a geometric figure of a synthetic and symbolic character.

Thus, a certain person who for a long time was dedicating herself to self-observation dreamed of a perfect square. She quickly perceived that this was a message from the superior mental and remained tranquil, although she had understood nothing. She attuned, however, in a special way with the picture of the dream, reaffirming mentally that she was linked with the inner source from which the figure came.

Then next she dreamed of a rectangle. Observing it, she noted that it did not have the purity of the picture in terms of vibration, because two of the sides were longer than the other two. Thus the rectangle did not transmit the same idea of order. She quieted herself, visualizing mentally the picture and the rectangle and remaining before them. Moments after, there emerged the following revelation in her consciousness: "The rectangle is you, not perfectly balanced; when in total alignment it is you as this square." Immediately she found that the energy of equilibrium permeated her as a kind of silent message, but very clear, so that it seemed to tell her: "transform your four sides into completely equal sides." This was an unforgettable stimulus for her.

In experiences such as this one we can perceive the difference between a mental dream which brings a purer evolutionary energy and the common dream, a mere extension of daily life. If with aspiration we are able to transcend the situations in our daily life (although we will live them with attention and love) and turn our mind to more spacious levels, these contacts will become possible.

There will begin, in this way, the arising in our life of another kind of dream. It can never be repeated too much that aspiration for spiritual progress is the core element of the whole process. This energy stimulates in a direct way all the cells, in all the bodies of the being. Therefore it is about a serene aspiration without ambitions, turning to the highest or to the depths of the being.

Teachings through dreams

If we compare our identity in the state of waking with that which is revealed in dreams or with that which is manifested in our deeper sleep, we will see that they are very different. Gradually we will discover the identity that is the truest. With regards to this, I here remember a biblical dream: the one that Joseph had in Egypt.

He was in the fields gathering straw with his brothers. When the work was finished, he saw the bundle of straw that he had prepared was standing vertically towards the sky, while the other bundles that represented the brothers prostrated themselves before the bundle that represented him, Joseph.

When he recounted this dream to his brothers they were astonished, because during waking they did not like Joseph, even hating him. However, in the dream bowing before him, his identity differed from that which he expressed in the day by day.

•••

Another typical case is that of a timid person, with little self-confidence, who did not have consciousness of his true inner reality. He asked for light with respect to himself in order to discover who he was. Soon after he dreamed of a long table upon which was a newborn bird with very few feathers. He was curious about this little bird, and in the dream he asked how to take care of it and what he could provide to keep it alive. Then there appeared a tall being, telling him that what was important was not to take care of the little bird; what was fundamental was that the bird had finally been born. "But what species of bird is it?" he asked the being. "It is a swan" he answered.

Esoterically the swan could be a symbol of the higher self, as in this case. It is as if the higher self already had been born in order to control the personality, although in the waking state there were still no clear signs of this.

•••

We cannot easily know the identity that we have in deep sleep. This effort induces us to dis-identify ourselves from our external personality and its reflections that usually appear in dream. In this way we see that our external and personal existence is like a type of construction. It is as if the being that lives in the deepest level, which we generally do not have consciousness of, when trying to manifest itself were building external figures. When projecting itself, it produces the identity of dream; after, projecting itself even more externally, this becomes our psychological identity, what we are outside.

The external identity, the personal I, is the more ephemeral and mutable identity. We lose the consciousness of it as soon as the body sleeps. If we did not wake up we could live without it. In dream, or in deep sleep, it is as if it never had existed.

Consequently, in dreams we can be more faithful to our deeper being. Because we are not completely incarnated in our physical brain while asleep, we have more freedom to be what we actually are. We can be whatever we want because time and space are different and locomotion is instantaneous. When we identify ourselves with this second (i.e. dream) phase of the projection of the true self, we begin to be less inhibited and more free.

Therefore, the person who dreamed with the swan perceived something that would not have been possible to notice in the waking life: that the higher self was born to conduct his personality.

If someone had revealed this reality to him he would not have believed it, because he did not have any external signs of it. But the dream transmitted to him trust and the possibility to recognize his own faith.

•••

I learned then, that if a dream comes from a higher level and shows what has to be done, what it brings is generally the opposite of what we would humanly do. Although it will seem strange to the common personality, together with this awareness comes the courage and the force to do what must be done, according to that which was seen in the dream.

As I have already said, about thirty years ago I had a circle of friends very different from what I have now. It was a strong circle, an intense life. It was difficult for me to conceive that this situation would change one day, as it seemed so real to me in the level of the personality. I decided, however, to seek clarification regarding this way of life that I was feeling was crystalized, and here is the dream that I had: a great swimming pool full of dirty water came before my eyes. Suddenly the water began to drain out of the pool, and in an instant it became empty and clean. The tiles, clear blue, became dry as if there never had been water there inside. Soon after clean water, crystalline, rose up to the edge of the pool and everything was shown very clearly to my consciousness.

This dream revealed to me the following: the swimming pool with the dirty water must be emptied by me and represented the old group of friends; the clean water that rose up was a new environment, a new circle of relationships that would come soon after I had freed myself from the old.

Upon awakening, I became aware of this message and I did not hesitate to separate myself from all that I knew. And the inner force did not stop there: it brought me to a distant country, gave me another profession, much more aligned with the times to come, and the people from the past did not look for me anymore, or if they had tried, they didn't find me. Time passed and they forgot me. Only after some years some of them reappeared, and even so, sporadically. Others came to look for me for spiritual reasons.

•••

Soon after I began to dedicate myself to study the dream life, I was very much helped by a well-informed person in this area who had a deeper knowledge of symbols. Perceiving that I was facing a rare opportunity, I imagined how good it would be if I could dedicate myself exclusively to this work for a while. After this I, who until now had lived occupied all day long, found myself living alone in a good location near the house of the instructor and with all my time free and available. It would have been impossible to understand with the rational mind how this could happen, but this is how it happened.

During this time of total dedication to the study of dream, as I did not have a fixed schedule for waking up, I could experience all kinds of dreams – those of the night, those of falling asleep and those which come after we awaken and we go back to sleep. Thus I had the opportunity to study them, sometimes on the same day, with that precious being…. I perceived that my karma was adjusted as a result of a correct aspiration and other changes also came in addition.

If we are really interested in becoming conscious of the dream world, the higher energies, which are omnipotent, will give to us the clarity and the necessary means to do so, in all levels. I affirm this based on my own experience.

•••

It is good to emphasize here that clarity does not come to the external eye only through dream. Actually, after passing through deep sleep and then being awake in the physical plane and remaining quiet and receptive, I can perceive that something 'has been implanted' in my consciousness. After this, I have a change of state. In moments such as this, there does not appear any voice, any vision, nothing. It is as if something indestructible is approaching. It cannot be named or explained. It is simple, something that comes. Without hesitation, I chose to contemplate this mystery.

For some people it is not easy to remember their dreams or to have mystical experiences. There are those who frequently do not remember them and there are those to whom they are completely unknown. However, even if it is not possible for someone to remember their dreams, all of us pass through them at least for two hours each night.

A greater or lesser tendency to remember dreams or to have mystical experiences depends on the psychic and cerebral mechanism of each person, and it also depends on other circumstances that are more or less impermanent. In addition, this ability often depends on karmic factors. The presence or absence of this tendency must not condition us or impress us. What is more important is the faith in the inner world, in the reality within us that exists and acts.

In the center of our being there is a powerful creative energy and part of it is evident in our oneiric life – where the impossible happens. To make the link between all the states in which we live – the waking state, the sleep state, the dream state, and the state of the deepest sleep – this is the challenge that is presented to us, especially in this epoch in which the development of the human mind permits it to assume the place of being an intermediary between the common consciousness and the superior consciousness.

To the extent that the human mind becomes silenced, it fulfills its evolutionary function.

The quality of dream life

Once, I was talking with a friend who had a very emotional nature, about an issue that is difficult to talk about in normal circumstances. However, to my surprise it was remarkable at that time how well the conversation flowed. The more that we spoke about this unusual issue, everything was perceived naturally by her, as if that which we were approaching was already known. When we finished, I told her: "Interesting, everything that we spoke about seemed familiar to us, as if within us it already existed."

She then commented that she had a dream with me the night before. In the dream, I promised her to speak about something, and soon after I invited her to: "Let's go up." The dream picture disappeared and the dream finished without her having the opportunity to have consciousness of what happened "up there." She told me that the part of the dream which she remembered was colorful and that the scenery of it seemed to be real, as if it were a reproduction of her home.

This event was very interesting because, while she lived this rapid dream experience, I was sleeping in the other room. Our consciousnesses evidently found each other and communicated with each other during the night. And from this communication surfaced our understanding. The conversation on the physical plane, the next day, was merely a reflection of that which had happened in the subtle level. But she did not have consciousness of our contact because it took place in the mental ("up there") and she was not able to perceive it.

In the beginning of her dream, while everything was colored and similar to the physical life, we were in the astral plane; the words "let's go up" signified that the contact would continue, however one level higher, i.e. in the mental. Having spent the day being emotional with a series of events, in the night she was not able to be conscious in another plane, as she is able to do most of the time.

Both in the state of sleep as in the state of waking, our activities change from one level to another, even when we are spiritually conscious. Sometimes the body sleeps and we remain lucid in the astral, losing the consciousness of the physical without thereby becoming conscious of the mental, as was in the case described. After the astral body ends its activity on its own level, there is the beginning of another activity, that of the mental body. These changes may occur many times during sleep. If each time that an activity ended in one of these planes, we could awaken and polarize our attention in the subsequent phase and then sleep again then we could deliberately go there and also be able to remember everything that transpired in the night. However, that which usually happens is that with this change, when we wake up in the morning we do not have consciousness of where we were and what remains imprinted in the brain is the minimal part of what took place with us.

If the consciousness is too much polarized in the dense material world, it is difficult to leave the physical body while it is asleep; if the emotions of the life of waking imprison us, during sleep we cannot go beyond the astral and the emotional planes.

•••

It is possible to perceive if a dream is a mental or an astral kind of dream. When it is more concrete in its images, and more similar to the life in the physical plane, the greater is the probability that it is an astral dream. This is not to say that a mental dream or even a spiritual dream cannot be a sharp, clear, or a true experience, but only in subtle levels.

Other evidence for the identification of the type of dream is the following: if in the dream, we can touch any object with the fingers very concretely, it indicates that this action is taking place in the astral plane or even in the etheric. Everything that is perceived by the physical senses: the smells, the sounds, indicates that the dream is near to these planes. As we reach levels more elevated, we perceive that everything can remain equally clear, however not with the same degree of materiality – and we are facing another sense of the real.

I will share something that shows how, for example, the dimensions of the etheric plane are similar to the physical. Some correspondence was sent to me by mail, and hours before arriving into my hands, I perceived it being placed under the door of the room where I sleep. This happened to me when I woke up in the morning, when I was in the liminal state between sleep and waking. It seemed to me to be a real concrete letter – only that the material was more porous, the kind which we see in pictures made with a magnifying lens and in which it is possible to see all the details. That which was placed under the door in the dream came from the mental plane of the individual who had sent the letter, passing through the etheric so that I could capture it before it arrived to the concrete plane. The image projected by this person was so close to that of the physical world that when I woke up, I had to look very clearly to be sure that there was nothing there. The concrete physical letter arrived during the day, and everything that I had passed through before prepared me to receive the written message, which was very important for me.

•••

Another observation to be made is that, in the mental plane dreams do not have color. We cannot say that they are white or black, because it is a kind of white or black that we do not know of in the physical plane. As we go up the levels of consciousness, our dreams increasingly lose similarity to what occurs in the physical world.

Esoteric books speak of the colors in the subtle levels, but in terms of impressions and inner vibrations, and not in the terms that we experience in the concrete life. Theoretically, it is impossible to describe them, because human words cannot express that which occurs in the more elevated planes of consciousness. It will be possible for the inner experience of colors to be experienced by all of us in a near future, and ultimately it will be part of the evolution of humanity.

•••

By developing in the physical world the consciousness of being a spectator of our own actions, feelings and thoughts, we begin to have this also in sleep. We can then see ourselves dreaming, which sometimes allows us to modify the end of an episode. For example, if we are dreaming that we are going to a certain place, we could intervene and if we wanted, make the body that is acting change its direction. This, of course, happens only in the levels of the personality, because in the superior levels it is not possible to impose what happens.

In the spiritual level there are no divisions and, because of this, in it there is no psychological spectator, as is the case in the three well-known dimensions. As the consciousness is absorbed into the spiritual plane, it will perceive everything else as known within it, for example the thinker and the less subtle levels.

We speak of the levels of existence as if they were isolated one from the other, but we do this only in order to have better comprehension of them. In truth they are interconnected, interacting one with the other, and they constitute a whole. Our being is a unity and one day we will be able to perceive it. Therefore, the activities in these various planes may occur simultaneously, although we have the illusion that they are successive.

I knew someone who for many years studied the TREATISE ON WHITE MAGIC of Alice Bailey. In the final stages of this study, the explanation of the rules for initiation from the treatises were given to him in a 'waking dream.' One of the rules that is most complex for the concrete mind was clarified while he was taking a shower – as he himself told us, humorously. This happened not only because there were channels of communication between all levels, including the physical, but also because these channels were found to be unobstructed. The movements made during the shower did not impede the message from arriving to the brain, with total clarity.

Part II

Other Steps

> *"Any person who reaches
> a state in which to be awake
> is no different from to be asleep
> must protect this accomplishment.
> Our ability to do this
> depends on our degree of depth."*
>
> Huai-Chin Nan

The spiritual function of dreams

If we did not spend some time disincarnated, it would not be possible for us to live upon the earth, as this experience is necessary for a period of time in order for us to have more experience and the opportunity to serve. At a certain point we disincarnate so that new bodies may be constituted which are more adequate for the situations in which they will be acting. The higher self then makes its synthesis and prepares more favorable future conditions according to the karma that was woven by the human ego during the life on earth. Therefore, the period of disembodiment is fundamental for the renovation of the energies.

In the state of dream something similar happens, only to lesser degree, because its duration is only of a few hours. If the consciousness did not retire from the physical body and immerse itself in deeper levels, thus removing itself from receiving external influences, the continuation of life here would not be possible. We need this restoration at least every twenty-four hours.

Let us illustrate this with an image of a sponge soaked in water. The water is the astral-emotional material of the individual, and the sponge itself is its physical-etheric body. While the water is in the sponge, the water is separated from the general reservoir; but if we squeeze the sponge inside of the reservoir, the water revitalizes itself because it returns to integrate itself back into the totality. Later on, being reabsorbed by the sponge, the water will be in a state of re-composition that can keep the sponge always fresh, without becoming dry and also without putrefying. This is an image created by Rudolf Steiner, who dedicated his whole life to studies of the soul.

In the same way, the astral substance that returns to the physical-etheric body after sleep revitalizes all of it, because it has passed some hours in the general planetary reservoir, and who knows, even in the extra-planetary one, which is an even more healthy level. If the astral body stayed always circumscribed by the physical, without periodic exits, an unsustainable situation would be created, because it needs the experience of merging into its original environment. There it can remain comfortable inside of its particular laws. In the same way, the higher self needs to return to its own level, where is found the basic vitality that is transmitted to the external consciousness.

•••

The contact with the super-sensible worlds is indispensable in order that life may flow in the correct rhythm. We cannot only count on the external consciousness, what is called the consciousness of waking, because it is limited to the denser vibrations. For example, I could mention that I remember having once prepared, with so much dedication, a talk that I believed to be appropriate for a group. Fortunately, during the night before this work, I had a dream in the astral plane in which I saw broken and split in half the sandals that I had the habit of wearing. I could understand from this dream that the talk I had planned was inappropriate for this kind of audience.

In this case, although in human terms, all the requirements for the realization of the talk were ready, in another level of reality it was different, and this was reflected in that way in the astral plane. We see with this that if the astral and mental vehicles of the personality did not leave during sleep and did not enter into another plane of life, certain facts could not be perceived with the necessary clarity.

•••

We must be forewarned, however, that while we attribute great value to the life that we experience during sleep, and when we stimulate others to observe their own dreams, it is not our intention to escape from the life of waking or that of the daily reality. We are impelled to search in other levels for the necessary elements so that the reality of daily life is lived according to our inner truth, and not in opposition to it. It is easy for human life to go in directions other than what is real. This is the example of the talk that I was preparing in an improper way. If this had not been corrected in time, it could have created a negative karma for my conscious self, hindering future actions of the higher self on Earth.

For a few years during this incarnation I had a very significant experience with karma yoga, i.e., with the yoga of clearing the destiny. I had the intention to balance what could be possible in my human karma and then to be more free for service to the world in general, disconnecting myself from particular interests that take so much time. Because I concentrated myself on this intention, my human life began to change and new situations were presented, offering me the opportunity to rescue past debts by means of unconditional and disinterested service. During this period, I saw that if I had not been so well supported by a lucid life of dreams, I could not have correctly faced certain situations, those in which I did not have any experience.

When I made this intimate and deep offer I began to have instructive dreams every night that guided me and which showed me what should be transformed. Then with security, I surrendered myself to the indicated transformation. I learned in practice, that dreams can play an important role in our spiritual ascesis. I relate here one of them that seems to be particularly enlightening.

My consciousness found itself in an elevated point, in a type of a cinematic studio where there was a film team. From above I was observing the people working confusedly below. In this studio there was also a cable car. Suddenly from the same higher place where I was, appeared a small basket with a new-born, that quickly descended by the cable and which fell into the lower part of the studio.

The very rapid dream consisted only of this. I never forgot it. I could read into it with much clarity that if I continued with the activities which I was developing, this new-born aspect of myself was going to die, to descend a level. I did not hesitate to abandon the artistic profession that I had been involved with for ten years, and this helped me to allow myself to be more free from karmic ties. It is good to notice that, soon after I had to make this decision, there opened up for me opportunities to develop other creative activities in various areas, for which I hardly had time to adapt myself to the new situations that were emerging. Henceforth I lived by faith, and the restoration of the energies came as a consequence.

•••

We must be attentive when we have dreams that are a spiritual stimulus. They can be not only distorted by the material available in our own mind, which is unprepared for this kind of vibration, but also be prejudiced by the opinion of others who are not always receptive to the uncommon. It is therefore not a good idea to share this type of dream, unless the person to whom we relate it is in alignment with our spiritual process because the person is living consciously their own process. We must speak of our internal experiences only if we have a deeper reason to do so, and even then, only with the correct person. Otherwise their effect is diluted.

We may only do this if revealing it helps others or if the other person has the ability to clarify for us some detail that by chance has remained obscure. The ideal is to keep within our self the experience of these dreams. Furthermore, in the event that we are not secure about its meaning or its implications, it is prudent to be silent, since we run the risk of transmitting to the other our insecurity, which could be harmful.

To speak about an experience in a way that is inadequate, sharing it with anyone, blocks the flow of the spiritual energy of dreams. Another factor that disturbs this delicate process is to be so occupied with activities that the personality considers to be important, that we relegate to a secondary plane the life of dreams. With this illusion, we end up not giving proper value to this source of wisdom, which makes difficult the manifestations of the supra-conscious.

•••

If each time that we are confronted with a physical, emotional, or mental problem we keep the doors open for the superior consciousness, from there will arrive the solutions. We may illustrate this very well with the case of a student who asked a question from the depths of his heart and received from his father the answer through a dream.

Because of its great interest, I will relate here some of its antecedents. This student having dedicated a period of his life to harmonization of himself, then searched for an adequate place where people were dedicated to an authentic spiritual quest. Finding it, as soon as he arrived there he had this experience, which he considered to be the most important of his life, because this experience introduced him to the world of dreams. Above all, it was very significant for someone who had never concerned himself with things of this kind.

In the dream of the student, his father told him to read Chapter 38 from the book of Job in the Bible. Although he was not familiar with the Bible and did not have any idea of its structure, as soon as he woke up he opened it randomly looking for the recommended chapter. How much was his surprise not only when he came across it, but also that he there found a message completely appropriate for himself. It was enough, then, for him to search for a connection with the supra-consciousness, going to that equilibrated environment so that the superior mind could manifest itself in an unequivocal way. Now, in the chapter indicated, Job has an encounter with God (in the Bible at times the supra-consciousness is called God), that said to him that it is not possible for humanity to know everything, because this wisdom is infinite and it cannot fit inside of a person. In this book it also said that to reach wisdom the person needs to transcend their own human condition and to enter into a broader one, and then to penetrate into areas that the supra-consciousness embraces.

In Chapter 38, God asks Job: "But, how could you, a human creature and therefore with a limited capacity, know with surety the stars of the sky, the path of the wind, or to know how the rocks were made?" Such knowledge is not under the control of a human, especially a mere human, but it is in the domain of another energy to do this. Then many questions are asked of Job, among them: "Are you capable of controlling the rain: to ask the rain to stop, or fall, to know how many drops of dew are created each morning?" Evidently, Job could not answer affirmatively to any of these questions. Then

God said to him: "If you are not able to do this, how could you want to control me, how could you ask me why I do these things or why I do them in a certain way?" Job then, became aware that first he had to expand his consciousness so that he could come closer to God and to obtain thus the answers that he was searching for. However, God, infinite wisdom, was in Job; it was his supra-consciousness.

This experience, for a student who was accustomed to analyze, was really remarkable and changed him very much. His more profound being told him that there are answers that we can have and others that we cannot.

•••

Another type of impediment for us to relate correctly to our inner world is to consider ourselves as very important – which causes the superior mind to remain retracted in its own level. As a result of this, often we do not find the solution to a question, since we do not take the superior mind into proper account. "This is only a detail" – we think. "I am interested in things more broad and profound." However, everything has relevance for the supra-consciousness. I can, for example, be stimulated to close a door or open a window; for this I must have a reason, and also a deeper one, and one just as important as when I read Chapter 38 of the book of Job. When we think that it is necessary to search in the supra-consciousness only for what we choose, we make a mistake because actually everything is essential.

•••

Also, the fact that we live according to formulas and schemes that are very familiar and which we are accustomed to, can impede us from receiving the light from the superior levels of our being. The supra-consciousness always sends orders to us in the form of unexpected information, as for example, the one to order someone to open the Bible to a specific chapter, without them ever having read it, or even having turned the pages. The truth is that our senses will prefer to remain with what is obvious, and this attitude pushes us away from superior contact which, in turn, does not hold on to what is older, or known.

If we become afraid of the unusual that comes from the supra-consciousness, if we judge it to be absurd, we close the door to its influence. We have to accept everything with naturalness, whatever it may be.

•••

In truth what will help us to understand a spiritual message is to remain in silence before it, imperturbable, loyal and above all quiet, whether the meaning is manifested or not.

I think that there is still another fundamental condition in order for us to penetrate the spiritual reality naturally: it is for us to fix our attention on it as our ultimate and single goal. In general, we become involved with the events of daily life and we end up giving more importance to them than to the search for self-knowledge. However, there is nothing more necessary and vital than to know what we are and what we have to do at each moment.

The sentence attributed to Mohammed is meaningful: "If someone tries to come the width of a hand closer to Me, I come an arm's length towards them, and if someone tries to come closer to Me by an arm's length, I come two arm's lengths towards them; if someone walks towards Me, I run to them." In fact, each time that we search for these superior worlds we obtain from them a response in this proportion. And in truth, when we come to think about opening ourselves to these dimensions it is because the energies from there have been attracting us for centuries . . .

•••

Let us consider an example. A spiritual and well-intentioned man wanted to visit a brother who lived in another city. Before going, he started to have doubts about whether he should indeed make this visit, if it was really necessary. Before sleep, there came to his mind the idea to ask the deeper levels about this. In response he dreamed of two dining tables placed side by side in a well-ventilated room. The table on the left was covered with a white cloth and was prepared for a celebration; the one on the right was empty. This dream came to him with great force, highlighting, above all, the table on the right as if it were the more important one.

The superior energies in the individual manifested clearly that he should not disperse himself; so much so that the table prepared for the normal visit, the social, the usual, was on the left. It is as if it were saying: "This table is beautiful, with a cloth, dishes and everything but it is on the left side" (the side that represents for the individual, the personality.) "Therefore, prepare yourself for a simple visit, without preconceived ideas. Strip your mind, and allow to happen what needs to happen."

The person understood, then, that the visit would be useless if it was not done well, and that if he decided to go, he should not bring his own ideas about what to discuss. If he would remain as a bare table, he would be provided by the spirit with the food that in the moment would best contribute to the evolution of all.

The evolutionary dream

Here we are dealing with dreams that result from the contact with the soul, both for those who are beginning to experience them, as well as with those who have had experience with them for a long time. Such contact establishes itself gradually to the extent that the purification of the personality is realized, and it presents itself according to the energy of the Ray of each soul, i.e. according to its nature.

As we have said before, this kind of experience that we call dream may happen not only during sleep, but in any moment of inner quiet. Normally the individual receives a message from the soul when it retreats into the cardiac center, and not when it is polarized in the emotional or lower levels. The region of the chest, in its occult sense, is a zone of consciousness and represents the life of the soul.

After a dream that has spiritual value there is always a change in the consciousness of the individual: he or she enters into a subtler state and feels transformed.

•••

Another characteristic of this type of dream, beyond its results in the cleansing of the consciousness, is that its significance is revealed immediately. It is so clear that further reflections are dispensed with. With regards to this, we can mention here the case of a doctor who demonstrated altruistic tendencies and who was preparing himself to enter into a life of spiritual service in his field of work. Then his human life began to pass through modifications that brought him to live alone, in order to not be occupied with anything other than to turn inside to the discovery of the inner world and to practice medicine. At this point, his brother, who was disoriented and who did not consciously follow any spiritual path, asked him if he could live with him. The doctor did not know what answer to give and, speaking with others about this issue, he received the suggestion to ask his inner being for an indication. It would be a risk for him to stop his work on perfecting his own concentration and on the creation of the necessary conditions for him to serve in a broader way, to simply comply with – for reasons of an emotional and sentimental nature – an individual request of doubtful origin.

The dream that came was very enlightening. It had a row of houses and one of them was indented, without being aligned with the others. Each of these houses represented one vertebrae of his spine. If another person who was not aligned with the inner work was to live in the house that was his, the alignment of the energy there would be disturbed.

•••

Other types of souls use the energy of will power over its vehicles. I can cite the example of a woman who had a well-developed family life and who used to do initiatic spiritual work, having under her orientation a group of people of different tendencies who were ready to take important spiritual steps. For this reason, it was fundamental to not have a life directed towards the external, but to give an example of another type of relationship with the world. And so, once between the states of sleep and waking, this woman saw the roof of her home crack and in that moment she knew that it was necessary for her to leave from there as soon as possible. However, this was so unexpected that she doubted if she had accurately captured what was in the dream. She did not have doubts regarding the will of her supra-conscious and she would be ready to leave her husband and children, but she felt that the way in which she had captured the dream could have been faulty. Because of this, she asked for confirmation regarding what she had seen.

The next morning she dreamed, in an equally clear way, of gate that was closing. The message was clear: "Either you pass through before the gate closes, or you will stay locked inside." One more time, she felt inclined to follow the recommendation of the message. However, she asked for another confirmation, still doubting her own human mechanisms. On the following day, her dream was of the funeral of the husband and some details of it demonstrated that it was a death of a moral nature. There were no more doubts that the supra-conscious will wanted her to be outside of the home. Then, at lunch time she shared with the family that she would be moving out that afternoon. She moved after that to a little apartment in the same city that, in some inexplicable way, had been unoccupied for many years.

Her friends and those who knew her thought that she was mentally unwell, and as time passed on, the less they understood her behavior, because her external relationships with her husband and children continued normally, with weekly visits from them to her apartment. At times the husband suggested that she could come home but the message had marked her so much that she did not see any possibility to go back. In addition to this, she passed through a deep change, and despite the permanence of these customary external contacts, it was as if she were in another phase of her incarnation. After this test, her consciousness was ready, as never before, for new experiences.

And this was what happened. Henceforth, there occurred transformations that the normal mind could never have imagined. The opportunity arose for a trip outside of the country and somewhat later, the change of her home to a neighboring country where economic developments allowed here to have a different rhythm of life. Finally, after all these changes, a national scandal exploded in which the husband was implicated. Therefore, if she had still been in his company during the period in which he had been involved in an illegal situation the people under her guidance, unable to perceive that she was not engaged with the situation, would have had their evolutionary process paralyzed or had to transfer important steps to a future life. However, with all that had happened it was confirmed that the continuity of the spiritual process, due to the urgency of the times, was important both for her, who had decided to keep herself free of this type of human karma, and for the souls who were following her.

In this way, this person continued her group spiritual work and, free from certain karmic contingencies, had her field of action more and more free in the years that followed. This shows that the action of the soul takes into account the evolution of the group and that the groups expand as the service is performed. A simply local work expands itself to a national, continental and finally a global scope.

•••

Bruno, the Carthusian monk, a well-known European historic personage from the year 1000, was one of the main counselors of the Pope, but the time had come for him to enter into a broader work than the mere business of Rome. Then, one morning he decided to abandon his responsibilities and asked the Archbishop for permission to go up to the Alps with six other companions, there in the heights in zones inaccessible to the curiosity of the world, to found the first Carthusian nucleus. Not by coincidence, on that same morning the Archbishop had had a dream with a sword pointing to the highest point of the Alps, in whose sky was shining a star of seven points. The permission was immediately given and sometime after, the Order of Carthusians became a world reality.

Dreams or visions of this nature can imprint themselves on the external consciousness of the being, without needing to cross the mental and emotional planes. They come from the level of the soul and they can register themselves directly in the physical brain without interferences. For this reason they are unequivocal, and whoever experiences them has no doubts about following them, although, as I affirmed earlier, they may bring unusual suggestions or instructions.

•••

Once I passed through an experience of this nature. I was coordinating a spiritual community and everything indicated that my physical presence there would be necessary for a long time. However, a vision came to dissolve this illusion of the personality. One morning, at the moment when I was waking, I saw the ring of keys that I used to enter the community headquarters thrown to the ground outside of the door. The image came directly from the supra-mental and I did not have any doubts: against all logic, I gathered the members of the group a few hours later and I told them about my departure. Taking only the time needed to arrange the minimum luggage necessary, I moved from there and I tried to erase all memories connected with that phase of my life. After this event, a totally new path opened up for the group and for myself.

•••

To the extent that we deepen the study of dreams they begin to refer, more and more, to the work of groups and to issues of a greater scope. Beyond this, the way in which spiritual dreams present themselves also progresses, because they follow the energy that envelops the planet and this is modified in each cycle. If we compare the historic dreams from the epoch of Atlantis, many of which are documented in the Old Testament, with those of the subsequent following epochs, we see in the latter, more recent, much more joy and satisfaction and less and less of a psychic atmosphere characteristic of the stages that have passed. Modern spiritual dreams are almost always clean, joyful, synthetic and constructive.

There are more people prepared for this kind of evolutionary dream than we could imagine. A student recounted, in her books, that her "guardian angel", which she usually saw in the superior levels of light, had a good sense of humor and presented to her, now and then, funny lessons in the form of dreams. Once, the angel made her dream with a reluctant boy, stubborn and unfriendly, "a little nuisance," so that she could recognize in this symbol her own personality that usually gave so much work to her "guardian angel." After this, she was more receptive to the counsels of the "angel."

To have a good sense of humor when facing one's own defects is a condition for the mental and emotional bodies to be unobstructed and to allow the pure message of the soul to pass through them.

Dreams as messages of the soul

Four individuals wanted to see a very famous symbolic tree. Someone who knew it very well offered himself to conduct them to it, one at a time. He brought the first during the winter, when the tree had only its trunk and branches, as all the leaves had fallen. Sometime later, he brought the second and, because it was spring, the leaves were beginning to appear. After this, during the summer, he brought the third and this person saw the tree flourishing. Finally, in the fall he brought the fourth one, who saw it full of fruits.

After these visits, the guide gathered the four people and asked them to describe the tree. The first said that he was surprised that the tree was so famous, because he did not see anything in it besides bare branches. The second said that the tree was just a normal tree with only a few leaves, but without any remarkable qualities. The third one said that the tree was so beautiful, with flowers full of life, and the fourth said that the tree really deserved the fame that it had: its fruits were copious and of great value.

There are those who refer to this story to illustrate how the common mind sees in a partial way. At each moment things change, they are not the same, and even so the mind continues defining things according to what it is capable of apprehending with its meager resources. The soul, on its part, knows that nothing is fixed, and when it speaks with us, it demonstrates the universality of its perspective. When it gives us a signal about something, it gives it in a synthetic way. In the case of the tree, the soul would see at once the diverse states of the plant complete and purified from the superfluous.

When we are free from the control of the physical brain, and therefore in a condition to penetrate broader realities, the everyday attitude with which we see situations disappears. By means of dreams, we know a world that our common senses cannot gain access to.

One time, I visited a group that was doing a spiritual work of a global scope, and I had a strong reaction to the customs and habits of its members. They deviated from the pattern of any work of this nature. I was very affected by what I saw and I asked that, in dream, the deeper reality of what was passing there could be shown to me. It was not long after, with the eyes closed and body relaxed, that I perceived a powerful space-ship of a type that I could never imagine was possible, immense in the sky. The sound that it made was minimal in comparison with its size. Coming back to the state of being totally awake, there came to me the understanding that this work, although demonstrated to be corrupted in the physical plane, still had with its energetic vibration enough force to transport thousands of souls to much higher levels of consciousness. And in reality this was the purpose of this group, not to create a form of perfect life in the physical plane, but to raise consciousnesses to the more elevated planes that they could reach. This was achieved by the radiation of the place where the group was installed and by nuclei in the air. Such radiation persisted despite the strange behavior of the members of the community. Therefore, the normal and critical mind, judging appearances, would never have had the conditions to have seen this.

•••

In order to communicate with us, the soul utilizes elements from our own memory. Thus, a symbol perceived by an individual generally is appropriate only for them. If I see a symbol and ask a normal analyst to interpret it, I may receive very diverse and interesting readings of the symbol. However, the shorter and more certain path, without a doubt, is to silence myself before what I see, to bring myself to the center of my being and to wait for the meaning to come from there. This is because on some occasions, the soul uses symbols that speak regarding our experience in previous lives. In this case only we ourselves have access to the true meaning of them.

Once the coordinator of a small meditation group asked for inner orientation with respect to two people interested in participating in the weekly meeting. In response, he had the vision of two compartments linked to each other, which he had never encountered in this life. In one of them, on the right, was one of the candidates, on the left the other. Suddenly the two compartments became separated and the one on the left was in the darkness. This vision served to reveal to him who should enter into the group and who should not be admitted.

All of this picture evoked in him, in addition, the intuitive impression that there was an unresolved obstacle between the two candidates and also probably between one of them and the group. The image, the symbol with a specific meaning for the person who saw it, made it clear that it was about a problem from past incarnations that was still influencing events in the present moment.

•••

It is fundamental to observe that messages from the soul do not contain judgments. In the example above, in showing two separate environments – one of which was in darkness – there is no critical judgment and no one was being condemned. The fact was shown simply, without even a small commentary. The soul does not say if one candidate is better than the other and does not point to anything that marks a person in an indelible way. Apparently it does not create karma in the same way that the conscious being does.

At the level of the human mind, this same message will be contaminated with a judgment of the event or of the two people involved, which will create karma for the mind and for the ego. The soul says "no" without giving out any concept: there is only a room in the darkness, possibly due to the vibration of the area shown and not by an action of the soul, which maintains itself impartial and apart in the face of this fact. These glimpses of the higher self are clear and pure and, to the extent that we receive them, we learn to transmit impulses without hurting or imposing conditions on others.

As is evident, the form of action of the soul is different from the form of action of the personality, but the latter can learn a new ethic by means of dreams or visions sent from the superior levels. My vision regarding the space-ship, for example, contained an important message which was "don't judge" and that it would not be proper to evaluate this group and its style of life. So, what the message taught me was "to not judge," because any judgment does not correspond to reality. The personality evaluates on the basis of its own experience, at times limited to the facts of the present incarnation. The soul, because it brings with it the experience of all previous incarnations and the wisdom of the same level in which it lives, shows a picture that takes into account a much broader and comprehensive perspective of creation and of the world than the mind can conceive. When it shows that a person is in the darkness, the soul does this without excluding it from the totality of life and without exempting us from our responsibility for what is happening with the person. Being that life is a totality, there are no alien situations that are of no concern to us, and neither is there an act of ours – physical, emotional or mental – that does not reflect positively or negatively upon others.

This is the universal point of view of the soul. If we are receptive to it, we will learn to be more open-minded and compassionate.

•••

Regarding all that has been said above, we can see how important is the work of not letting ourselves be impressed by what we perceive in our waking lives. The less we let ourselves be influenced by the material senses, the more we approach the reality of the soul, which includes other kinds of senses, i.e. the internal, and in addition its own.

In a certain phase of my relationship of long standing with a professional colleague, this abstraction from the external senses had great importance. When this old friend from so many lives, presented himself in this incarnation he appeared in a physically and psychologically precarious situation. In a talk that we had, he told me that he was going to abandon the university, leaving incomplete his course in medicine that could in the future serve as an instrument of beneficial action of his soul upon innumerable people whom he would encounter in future phases of his life on Earth. In the first moment of our talk he revealed his external and human situation, and if I had not been able to abstract myself from everything that he was saying and from what my senses were perceiving, I could not have realized the nature of his real situation. In the subtle levels it was shown to me, by a dream that I had the day following the meeting, that he would be a great doctor: he was radiating curative energy and before him was a straight and magnificent path. After this dream he returned other times and we studied together various themes until finally, his confused phase had passed. Everything was overcome and the plan of the soul, projected in his unobstructed mind, prevailed.

There is then, the need to not let ourselves be guided by any appearance, no matter how obvious it could seem to the common mind, in order to be receptive to the message that comes from levels where perfection is the reality in all of us.

After having made the choice to follow the will of the soul, my friend also had a dream, written down as follows: "I dreamed that I was entering a house that had many rooms, one after another, with doors of communication between them. In the first room there was an enormous confusion, the second was a little better, the third was less dense and the last one was much more organized. Thus, I was passing from one to another as if I was leaving from one phase for the next, until I arrived at a place in the house which opened into a new section of it. There was a door through which could pass only those who were meant to be 'saved' (this was the expression used), and those who could not enter were to stay there."

The scenes in this dream, according to what we could perceive, represented a type of test that was taking place on Earth. As the protagonist passed from one room to another, he was feeling more and more secure, until he arrived in the last room which contained only a rectangular table where two or three people were waiting for him for a purpose that had not been revealed.

With the reception of this message, my friend was able to finish the university, and even with all the crises that he faced there, he followed the path that the symbols had indicated, and today he has the ability to help many to harmonize and balance themselves. He is no longer identified with the psychic confusion that reigns in our surroundings.

•••

Currently the conditions of the Earth encourage souls to be clear in the transmission of their objectives. One of these objectives that is a goal for the soul is the correct use of energies: they must be expended only if they will be used in the best way. At present all energy is precious because of the great general need of help and equilibrium. Economy of force is so fundamental for us to be useful, that the higher self warns us when we do not observe it. At times sentimentality and social convention bring us to compromise with people and situations that harm our goal, thus becoming instruments of a wasting of energy. I had an experience of this type when I received a signal from my higher self that immediately clarified a situation for me. There appeared in my life two people who were emotionally involved with me and with my work; I asked to my inner being if this contact was beneficial and if I should maintain it. The answer came to me almost immediately as a dream with an electric plug that was disconnected.

•••

In our search for clarification, there are two processes that we can use, depending on which offers the least resistance for us. In the first we ask the inner world about what we need to know. In the second we simply open ourselves to its orientation without asking anything. Sometimes I use one and other times the other. If for example, I ask a question and I don't obtain an answer, I remain in a quiet state of listening. In some way a message always comes, sometimes even through the external facts that take place soon after.

If we see everything in a positive way, in the end we will apprehend the real. It is important to have clarity that the characteristics of our process of contact with the inner are not permanent but rather, are mutable. It could happen that in a past life we had an intense experience with dream, with visions or perceptions of all kinds, which could bring us to a phase of rest in this lifetime that makes it possible to make adjustments in our being. Then, to stop dreaming for a time could even be therapeutic and thus, would not constitute a symptom that we are closed to this way of penetrating broader realities. On the contrary, as I have said, it could be a necessary phase for new adjustments. For many of those who lived in Atlantis in the past, the life of dreams today is limited to the minimum necessary in order for them to balance the excesses from that time.

The reality beyond dreams

Still, there exists an experience of a level more elevated that differs from dream and that is beyond it. This is what is customarily called *true vision*, i.e., what is not filtered by any human part of the being. We experience this in the same way as we do the dream, but without images and impressions. We have here a step beyond the reality that we are able to capture in dream.

This true vision is an experience that the soul has in its own level, independent of the bodies that it uses on Earth. For this type of experience, which is of a more advanced degree, the individual must already be conscious of the causal body – the body of the higher self. The individual then acts as the higher self and the external I is absorbed into this nucleus, coming to live imbued with the elevated consciousness of it.

Different people who have never communicated with each other reported to me similar experiences when they reached this phase. They told me that when these experiences became the nature of the higher self and divested of any visible images, they came into contact with the group which they were part of in deeper levels. This group exists beyond mental thinking, i.e., in the level of the higher consciousness of each one of us. One of these people told me that she perceived her group as a circle, with a being who was more advanced than the other members in the center, and that he was the instructor of the souls present there.

These are conscious souls whose human egos, in which they are incarnated, participate with their souls in the experience of the teachings that come from the master of the Ray. The Ray is the basic and potential energy that determines certain qualities and tendencies. Although the personality and their bodies also have their Rays, what is important for us in this kind of elevated experience is the manifestation of the will of the Ray, i.e. the basic energy of the higher self. The master of the Ray, who is the catalyzer of the higher energies, is who transforms the energies in order to distribute them to the group. He or she is the instructor who prepares these souls for subtle services to be done, sometimes on non-physical levels.

•••

There are individuals who, by means of this type of experience, recognize their inner group, whose members are not always incarnated in the physical world. The recognition of one's inner group and one's role within it will become more commonplace in the decades which are approaching and is part of the development of the souls of humanity.

The frontiers between a dream of a superior quality and a true vision are slight. It is not simple to define the limit between one and the other, and to establish the differences between the states of consciousness in question.

When the conscious self perceives the life of the soul, the inner group and the master, who represents the highest will, there is also the possibility to perform its tasks in the physical plane according to that which is 'learned' in the classes of this inner group. One person who called her group the *ashram* told me that she was learning to accomplish transmutations and that she was beginning to be able to transform in certain respects the karmic situation of humanity.

In addition, a friend who works in this way shared with me many examples of how it was not difficult to harmonize her two conscious lives: one of the dimension of the soul and the other that of its denser vehicles upon Earth. She is able to do this without her closer friends being aware of her double activity. She lives withdrawn in an area between mountains and she takes care of many pure-bred animals in her home. These animals have such advanced perceptions that, in the moment that my friend enters into contemplation, they surround her, to protect her from certain vibrations. The dogs transmute the forces that are contrary to her work, with audible sounds from their stomach; while the cats stretch themselves in a way that serves to liberate energy. It was beautiful to see two kingdoms of nature, the human and animal, together in the same work. The plants around also collaborated in the purification of the environment, thus supporting the development of a valuable service for the world, the service of transforming energies.

•••

Gradually, also in the level of the personality, we are being prepared to achieve these levels of consciousness. However, the human ego does not always participate in these experiences, as it may not be aware of this broader facet of its life. And dreams are the door for this comprehension for the individual who still has not entered the state in which it is possible to perceive with clarity life in its greater reality.

Still, one must be warned that the works developed by an inner group in benefit of planetary healing normally must not be revealed, because due to the present conditions of the world, any such information could awaken forces of reaction and of conflict with them. To reveal to the levels of the concrete mind what is passing in one of these *ashrams* would serve to expose a plan to the adverse forces. The experiences in the inner groups are conscious for the individuals who have control of thought to the point that they do not transmit them in any way – which is possible only for disciplined and pure minds. To these individuals, perfect control of the feelings is also necessary, as an emotional reaction during an experience of this nature could affect the physical health, which depends on what the etheric counterpart of the nervous system transmits. A reaction can produce conflicts of energies with subsequent illness or disorders in the physical body.

It is good to have in mind that true vision does constitute an adventure of the personality in higher levels of existence, as are certain dreams. It does constitute an experience of the soul revealed lovingly to the personality so that it, imbued with spiritual will, love, wisdom and intelligence, manifests in time all these qualities in the world in which it is situated.

Prophetic dreams

Preceding the phase called true vision there are prophetic dreams. Equally real and not motivated by the desires of those who dream, they may occur before the personality becomes firm and stable as a consciousness in the higher self, where the experience of meditation occurs.

Prophetic dreams may occur among normal people when the soul perceives the need to transmit something important to the vehicles which it inhabits.

In certain cases, the transmission of the prophecy comes about as a warning to the conscious I, as an indication that some basic behavior must be changed. In other cases, it is a call for the human ego to collaborate in a beneficial way in what is to come. There are also cases of a prophetic dream that comes only to prepare us psychologically for that which is coming, inevitably, to our field of experiences. Finally, this kind of dream could also point out that which we must avoid.

Let us see an example of a prophetic dream in which the conscious I was made aware regarding a possible karmic event. There are situations that may or may not come about depending on our attitude and behavior. In the case in question, the protagonist was staying in a hotel, and during the night he dreamed that an elevator operator in uniform pointed out a hearse to him. After awakening in the morning, with the dream strongly impressed in his brain, he prepared himself to leave and arriving in the hall, he called for the elevator. When the door opened up, the elevator operator in the cabin, in a normal gesture, pointed to the entrance. It was exactly the figure that had appeared in his dream indicating the hearse. Even the uniform was the same. In the face of this, the protagonist of the dream decided to not enter into the elevator and preferred to descend by the stairs, although there were many floors. When he arrived in the lobby, he saw a grouping of people in the entrance of the building, scared because the elevator had fallen.

We have here a typical prophetic dream delivered to the ego so that it could avoid the experience if it chose to, as it did. For the conscious I, it was a test of memory and of attention; if the memory had failed, if convenience had predominated (there were dozens of floors to descend by foot), or if the conscious I had not been attentive to the message, the personality would have passed through the experience of the physical fall of the elevator, with all of its consequences.

The higher self constantly tests the ego with the intention of making it agile and sharp, ready for a broader life. The human part of an individual must become adequate to act, feel and think in a creative way in the world of forms.

A well-known clairvoyant from the past presented a prophetic dream as an example, whose message was not listened to by the protagonist. It concerned a factory worker who dreamed that when he was carrying out certain tasks in the factory, he had his right arm decapitated by one of the machines. On the same day while all of the factory was in operation, the machine which he had seen in the dream failed. As soon as he knew about this he remembered the dream and he thought to leave the factory at that moment in order to not be called to fix it.

However, he didn't and soon after the supervisor came to bring him to fix it. At the beginning of the task, the machine gravely injured him in the same arm that in the dream had been amputated.

•••

We can also have premonitory dreams but these do not have the same degree of clarity as prophetic dreams. A premonitory dream carries within it a mixture of emotional elements sentiments, sensations, and sufferings. They generally originate from the astral level where events occur before their materialization on the physical plane. Prophetic dreams originate from a higher level, referring to the life of the soul and not to that of the personality.

A premonitory dream may leave doubts about its veracity but prophetic dreams are unquestionable: one who dreams them has the impression of "seeing" an experience which, in truth, will only come about later. The premonitory dream may sometimes scare the individual because they do not carry an energy adequate to support the dreamer or provide them with orientation in their crises. The prophetic dream, on the contrary, brings with it the courage and the ability to face any situation that has been announced as probable or certain.

The premonitory dream is only anticipating something that may or may not occur, while a prophetic dream brings to the personality discernment, reason and the capacity to make decisions. It is good to always be calm whether dealing with situations, whether difficult or happy, which are announced by premonitory dreams. It is not a good idea to allow oneself to be influenced by them, by feelings of either depression or euphoria.

•••

One morning I was very quiet and withdrawn after a night in which I had lived intense processes in my inner life. The personality was turned towards a deeper movement of transformation. All of a sudden, there arose before my inner eyes an enormous cement staircase. However, the steps were so narrow that in order to ascend them it was almost necessary to crawl. The passage from the first floor to the second was not easy, because there was a bricklayer there who would not look me in the eyes, and who was walling up the steps with rocks and cement. The wall that he was erecting seemed to be strong and insurmountable. If it had been finished, it would have been impossible to move to the second floor.

Then something unpredictable happened: the bricklayer disappeared and I came very close to the newly erected wall. With decisiveness I started to remove the obstacles that had been cemented and I perceived that they could be easily removed and also that they were not really fixed. They were heavy only in appearance and it was enough to touch them in order for them to be dislodged.

The more that I reflect about this dream, the more meanings I find, and now as I am reporting it, I revive it and I perceive new elements. Today I read it differently from on that morning and it speaks to me more than before.

Dreams, experiences, and quietude can be infinitely creative if we remain receptive to them...

A vision

As I stated in the beginning, as soon as I started being interested in dreams, opportunities opened up for me to study them in depth and the circumstances of my life began to change so that a concentration on this issue could be possible and so that no obstacles could remain between my being and the reality that was to unveil.

I remember that it was fall and that I was going up an avenue lined with trees up to an apartment building where I regularly studied dreams. On this afternoon, as I was approaching the place, I saw it as if it were new. It was as if I were there for the first time. I knocked on the door and as soon as it was opened I could even smell an aroma that I had never experienced before. Everything was new, on all levels, even on the physical plane already so well known.

When I entered into the studio, a magic place for me, I immediately saw a new painting with a shining tint and still fresh. My eyes could not stop looking at the scene for some moments. "When did you create it?" I asked to the painter. "This morning" was the answer. "I saw it in meditation and in dreams." I stayed there unmoving, receiving this impression, and a feeling of responsibility, a new vision, touched me completely. I asked him what was awaiting us, what was expected of us now. He answered me that it would depend on humanity, how it could react; if humanity would wake up for its true task on earth, that which was prophesized in the painting would only be partially realized; but if it did not awaken enough, the scenes in the painting would come about. In the upper part of the painting, as if coming down from the sky, a bluish white light flowed lovingly and permeated everything that was expressed with brush and paints. The light was there in some unconditional way, regardless of the choice that humanity would make.

In the painting, a land divided in half by a reddish river could be seen. On one side some people, bent over and without energy, could not pass to the other side. On the other side, the people had an erect posture and were occupied with group tasks, i.e., with a work of salvation. There were open cracks on the ground on both sides of the river. A dark smoke came out from the earth and was descending from the sky. But the constructive action continued, in spite of the arid desert which was being formed. In the background were visible other levels of consciousness, with the counterpart of these bodies (on either side of the river) in very different situations. The work was being done on all levels and it was possible for the same people to participate in many of these levels. There was more work than there were people to do it.

In the foreground, almost on the bank of the river, a human figure – pictured in a special form – helped another who was dying. From the whole scene there emanated a curative energy that spread equally over all, whatever the fate that each one might choose.

Glossary

ALIGNMENT – Harmonization between the bodies of the personality and between these and the higher self. In addition, there are alignments that are realized in more elevated levels. For alignment a whole work of purification is necessary.

ASHRAM – A word used in ancient times to designate an environment of devotees and yogis who followed a guru or spiritual instructor. Each guru had their ashram which manifested a specific vibration and which represented a certain Ray energy with the purpose of elevating humanity and the world. With the passing of time the ashrams were transferred from the physical plane to the dimension where the soul (or the higher self) has its life and its own consciousness. In these ashrams there is always a being more developed on the scale of evolution, already free from the incarnational cycle, giving instruction to a determined group of souls, incarnated or not.

ASTRAL or EMOTIONAL LEVEL – The dimension that corresponds to the feelings and emotional reactions. It is extremely fluid and mutable.

BODIES OF THE HUMAN – A series of vehicles that correspond to the different levels of energy that compose the universe and by means of which the true individual is manifested.

BODIES OF THE PERSONALITY – These are three: the etheric-physical, the astral-emotional and the mental-thinking. Each of them is in relationship, respectively, with the levels or states that have the same name. These bodies can function with relative independence and the three together constitute the personality. They become disintegrated after the higher self disincarnates.

CONSCIOUS SELF – The part in the individual that corresponds to the level of the personality. Restructured in each incarnation by means of a continuous development, the conscious self holds the synthesis of all previously lived experiences.

COSMIC CONSCIOUSNESS – The highest degree of unity that a human being can reach: illumination or transcendent realization.

CAUSAL BODY – This corresponds to the region of the abstract mind. It is the vehicle of expression of the higher self or soul. When the being disincarnates, it remains intact on its own level.

ESOTERIC PSYCHOLOGY – The study of transcendental realities still not known in their totality by modern science. This study brings the person to penetrate a more profound, inner level of consciousness. Being in relationship with the knowledge of the energies of the seven Rays, it especially seeks to help humanity to discover how these Rays are expressed, acting in each one of its bodies.

ETHERIC CENTERS OF THE BEING – The focus of life, energy, force and consciousness found in each plane of existence. The human being has many of these centers, each one of them performing a specific function in its development and in its relationship with the cosmos.

INITIATION – Expansion of consciousness that allows the development of superior faculties and conscious life in levels of elevated existence.

KARMA – A term linked to the law of cause and effect, according to which all action, feeling and thought produces effects of a similar nature that return to those who generate them. In other words, everything that we do, feel or think comes back to us, to their point of origin over a short, medium or longer time. We are accustomed to use the word "destiny" to substitute for "karma." However, the word "destiny" is not adequate to express it. We can observe that there is a basic karma that must be, in principle, totally accepted by the individual. Only after this initial acceptance is it possible to transform it. It is from this basic karma, which pre-exists the physical birth, that each being will construct a web of its own life and as a consequence modify its karma. We are creating our karma (positive and negative) without ceasing, and transforming it according to our attitudes, wishes, and aspirations. The work with karma is, as a consequence, continuous and its duration equals the period of our life upon Earth.

MENTAL LEVEL – The dimension that distinguishes a human being from an animal. It is subdivided into the concrete mental (or inferior thinking mind) and the abstract mental (superior mind).

PHYSICAL-ETHERIC LEVEL – The more dense level of manifestation. It is composed of physical matter (solids, liquids and gases) and of their etheric counterpart, which permeates, shapes and vitalizes it.

PURIFICATION OF THE PERSONALITY – Removal of the obstacles to the attunement of the material bodies with the laws and rhythms of levels of superior consciousness.

RAYS – Currents of energy coming from the cosmos that demonstrate specific qualities. They are present wherever life is manifested, whether it be an atom or a person or a solar system.

SOUL or HIGHER SELF – The nucleus of our being that contains the perfect idea of the meaning of group, of universality, of higher love, of spiritual will and of intelligent activity. The higher self pre-exists and subsists after our life on earth.

SUBCONSCIOUS – The part of the consciousness in which are registered the experiences lived not only in the present incarnation but also in past incarnations, those which the consciousness does not remember. When this memory comes to the surface, it becomes integrated into the consciousness.

SUBTLE LEVELS – Levels of the consciousness that pass beyond the physical-etheric plane.

SUPRA-CONSCIOUSNESS – The part of the individual consciousness that is attuned with the cosmic consciousness. Its degree of amplitude is such that it passes beyond the limits of one's own higher self.

THOUGHT FORMS – The emanations of the mind of a human being or of more elevated entities that contain specific qualities. These emanations create forms that come into action and that integrate themselves with others, exercising influences according to their vibrations. When we generate thought-forms we are building our own karma.

TRIALS or TESTS – Situations and events that make purification possible for us according to our capacity to accept them and support them or transform them. By means of these trials we may access our physical, emotional, mental and physical strengths.

UNCONSCIOUS – The area of the being still not perceptible to the personality or conscious self. It covers both the supra-consciousness and the subconscious.

About Trigueirinho and his work

José Trigueirinho Netto (1931-2108) was born in Sao Paulo, Brazil. He lived in Europe for a number of years, where he maintained contact with individuals who were advanced on the spiritual path, including Paul Brunton.

In his own life he was an example of the teachings that he transmitted through books and talks about the transcendence and elevation of the human being, the contact with the soul and with even more profound nuclei of the being, impersonal service, and the link with the Spiritual Hierarchies.

One of the fundamental elements of his work is to stimulate the expansion of human consciousness and to liberate it from the bonds that keep it imprisoned to material aspects of existence, both external and internal.

He was the founder of the Figueira Community of Light *(https://www.fraterinternacional.org/en/life-in-the-light-communities/)* and one of the members of the Board of Directors of the Fraternity International Humanitarian Federation *(https://*

www.fraterinternacional.org/) and co-founder of the Grace Mercy Order. He also was an active collaborator, instructor and spiritual protector of three other communities located in Uruguay, Argentina and Portugal.

In his last 30 years he lived in Figueira, in the interior of Minas Gerais, Brazil, a community that at present has approximately 300 residents and which is visited by thousands of collaborators who are members of a network of humanitarian services and of spiritual studies, which was was always followed closely by Trigueirinho.

Thanks to his inestimable instruction and his love for the Kingdoms of Nature, and as a result of the exemplary work that he himself implanted in the Figueira community, the Animal, Vegetable and Mineral Kingdoms are the recipients of loving treatment there.

Trigueirinho wrote 81 books published originally in Portuguese with many of them translated into Spanish, English, French and German. He gave more than 3,000 talks that were recorded live and which are available in CD, with some available in DVD and pen drive.

The primary focus of the first phase of Trigueirinho's work was concerned with self-knowledge, prayer, instruction and spiritual transformation. Following this, he began to transmit information with respect to Universal Life and about the assistance that humanity has from the beginning received by means of the Intra-terrestrial White Brotherhood which inhabits the Retreats and the Planetary Centers and also through the Cosmic Brotherhood of the Universe. He also mentions the presence of the Spiritual Hierarchy on the planet and the advent of the new humanity.

His work also includes themes relating to: the need for humanity to balance the negative karma that it has created in relation to the Kingdoms of Nature; the negative karmic burden that we carry from the history of slavery and the genocide of indigenous peoples; and the nature of spiritual work in groups. He also addresses issues of healing, a larger vision of astrology, the esoteric nature of symbols, sound and colors, and the divine feminine.

In his last eight years he analyzed with clarity, and with the wisdom that always characterized him, the messages that the Divinity has been giving to the planet as a warning to humanity (available from www.mensajerosdivinos.org/en).

His work reveals a real comprehension of the significance of all the Kingdoms of Nature on our planet, the true spiritual task of the human being, its place in the universe and also its responsibility before Creation.

Finally, he clarifies the reasons for the crisis that today is devastating humanity, teaching us how to avoid reacting negatively to an immanent natural catastrophe by contacting more subtle levels of consciousness, and opening perspectives for the beginning of a more luminous cycle for our race.

Books by Trigueirinho

(Books available in English have English title first)

ORIGINALLY PUBLISHED BY EDITORA PENSAMENTO
Sao Paulo Brazil

1987

OUR LIFE IN DREAMS
NOSSA VIDA NOS SONHOS

A ENERGIA DOS RAIOS EM NOSSA VIDA
THE ENERGY OF THE RAYS IN OUR LIVES

1988

DO IRREAL AO REAL
FROM THE UNREAL TO THE REAL

Hora de Crescer Interiormente – O Mito de Hércules Hoje
TIME FOR INNER GROWTH – THE MYTH OF HERCULES TODAY

A Morte Sem Medo e Sem Culpa
DEATH WITHOUT FEAR OR GUILT

Caminhos Para A Cura Interior
WAYS TO INNER HEALING

1989

Erks – Mundo Interno
ERKS – THE INNER WORLD

Miz Tli Tlan – Um Mundo Que Desperta
MIZ TLI TLAN – AN AWAKENING WORLD

Aurora – Essência Cósmica Curadora
AURORA – COSMIC ESSENCE OF HEALING

Signs Of Contact
SINAIS DE CONTATO

O Novo Começo Do Mundo
THE NEW BEGINNING OF THE WORLD

A Quinta Raça
THE FIFTH RACE

Padrões de conduta para a nova Humanidade
PATTERNS OF CONDUCT FOR THE NEW HUMANITY

Novos Sinais De Contato
NEW SIGNS OF CONTACT

Os Jardineiros Do Espaço
THE SPACE GARDENERS

1990
A Busca da Síntese
THE SEARCH FOR SYNTHESIS

Noah's Vessel
A NAVE DE NOÉ

Tempo de Retiro e Tempo de Vigília
A TIME OF RETREAT AND A TIME OF VIGIL

1991
Portas do Cosmos
GATEWAYS OF THE COSMOS

Encontro Interno – *A Consciência-Nave*

INNER ENCOUNTER – *The Consciousness Space Vessel*

A Hora do Resgate
THE TIME OF RESCUE

O Livro Dos Sinais
THE BOOK OF SIGNS

Mirna Jad – *Santuário Interior*
MIRNA JAD – *Inner Sanctuary*

As Chaves de Ouro
THE GOLDEN KEYS

1992

Das Lutas à Paz
FROM STRUGGLE TO PEACE

A Morada Dos Elisíos
THE ELYSIAN DWELLING PLACE

Hora de Curar – *A Existência Oculta*
TIME FOR HEALING – *The Occult Existence*

O Ressurgimento de Fátima Lis
THE RESURGENCE OF FATIMA LIS

História Escrita nos Espelhos
Princípios de Comunicação Cósmic
HISTORY WRITTEN IN THE MIRRORS -
Principles of Cosmic Communication

Passos Atuais
STEPS FOR NOW

Viagem por Mundos Sutis
TRAVEL THROUGH SUBTLE WORLDS

Segredos Desvelados – *Iberah e Anu Tea*
UNVEILED SECRETS – *Iberah and Anu Tea*

A Criação – *Nos Caminhos da Energia*
CREATION – *On the Paths of Energy*

The Mystery of the Cross In the Present Planetary Transition
O MISTÉRIO DA CRUZ NA ATUAL TRANSIÇÃO PLANETÁRIA

O Nascimento da Humanidade Futura
THE BIRTH OF THE FUTURE HUMANITY

1993

Aos Que Despertam
TO THOSE WHO AWAKEN

Paz Interna em Tempos Críticos
INNER PEACE IN CRITICAL TIMES

A Formação de Curadores
THE FORMATION OF HEALERS

Profecias aos Que Não Temem Dizer Sim
PROPHECIES FOR THOSE WHO ARE NOT AFRAID TO SAY YES

The Voice of Amhaj
A VOZ DE AMHAJ

O Visitante – O Caminho Para Anu Tea
THE VISITOR –*The Way to Anu Tea*

A Cura da Humanidade
THE HEALING OF HUMANITY

Os Números e a Vidas – *Uma Nova Compreensão da Simbologia Oculta nos Números*
NUMBERS AND LIFE – *A New Understanding of Occult Symbolism in Numbers*

Niskalkat – *Uma Mensagem para os Tempos de Emergência*
NISKALKAT – *A Message for Times of Emergency*

Encontros Com a Paz
ENCOUNTERS WITH PEACE

Novos Oráculos
NEW ORACLES

Um Novo Impulso Astrológico
A NEW ASTROLOGICAL IMPULSE

1994

Bases do Mundo Ardente – *Indicações para Contato com os Mundos suprafíscicos*
BASES OF THE FIERY WORLD – *Indications for Contacts with Supraphysical Worlds*

Contatos com um Monastério Interaterreno
CONTACTS WITH AN INTRATERRESTRIAL MONASTERY

OS OCEANOS TÊM OUVIDOS
OCEANS HAVE EARS

A TRAJETÕRIA DO FOGO
THE PATH OF FIRE

GLOSSÁRIO ESOTÉRICO
ESOTERIC LEXICON

1995

THE LIGHT WITHIN YOU
A LUZ DENTRO DE TI

1996

DOORWAY TO A KINGDOM PORTAL PARA UM REINO

BEYOND KARMA
ALÉM DO CARMA

1997

WE ARE NOT ALONE
NÃO ESTAMOS SÓS

WINDS OF THE SPIRIT
VENTOS DO ESPÍRITO

FINDING THE TEMPLE
O ENCONTRO DO TEMPLO

THERE IS PEACE
A PAZ EXISTE

1998

PATH WITHOUT SHADOWS

CAMINHO SEM SOMBRAS

MENSAGENS PARA UMA VIDA DE HARMONIA

MESSAGES FOR A LIFE OF HARMONY

1999

TOQUE DIVINO

THE DIVINE TOUCH

COLEÇÀO PEDAÇOS DE CÉU

BITS FROM HEAVEN COLLECTION

- **AROMAS DO ESPAÇO**
  AROMAS FROM SPACE
- **NOVA VIDA BATE À PORTA**
  A NEW LIFE AWAITS YOU
- **MAIS LUZ NO HORIZONTE**
  MORE LIGHT ON THE HORIZON
- **O CAMPANÁRIO CÓSMICO**
  THE COSMIC CAMPANILE
- **NADA NOS FALTA**
  WE LACK NOTHING
- **SAGRADOS MISTÉRIOS**
  SACRED MYSTERIES
- **ILHAS DE SALVAÇÁO**
  ISLANDS OF SALVATION

2002

CALLING HUMANITY
UM CHAMADO ESPECIAL

2004

ÉS VIAJANTE CÓSMICO
YOU ARE A COSMIC WAYFARER

IMPULSOS
IMPULSES

2005

PENSAMENTOS PARA TODO O ANO
THOUGHTS FOR THE WHOLE YEAR

2006

TRABALHO ESPIRITUAL COM A MENTE
SPIRITUAL WORK WITH THE MIND

2009

SIGNS OF BLAVATSKY—AN UNUSUAL ENCOUNTER FOR THE PRESENT TIME
SINAIS DE BLAVATSKY –
UM INUSITADO ENCONTRO NOS DIAS DE HOJE

Published by Editora Irdin
Carmo da Cachoeira, Minas Gerais, Brazil

2012

Consciências e Hierarquias
CONSCIOUSNESSES AND HIERARCHIES

2015

Mensagens Reunidas
COLLECTED MESSAGES

Mensagens para Sua Tranformaçã
MESSAGES FOR YOUR TRANSFORMATION

2017

Páginas de Amor e Compreensão
PAGES OF LOVE AND COMPREHENSION

2018

Novos Tempos: Nova Postura
NEW TIMES: NEW ATTITUDE

2020

Versos Livres
OBRA PÓSTUMA

Trigueirinho's works are published by:

ASSOCIAÇÃO IRDIN EDITORA – www.irdin.org (selected titles of books in English and Portuguese and CDs in several languages), Carmo da Cachoeira, Brazil.

EDITORA PENSAMENTO – www.pensamento-cultrix.com.br (titles in Portuguese), São Paulo, Brazil.

EDITORIAL KIER – www.kier.com.ar (selected titles in Spanish), Buenos Aires, Argentina.

LICHTWELLE-VERLAG – www.lichtwelle-verlag.ch (selected titles in Spanish and German), Zurich, Switzerland.

SHASTI ASSOCIATION – www.shasti.org (selected titles in English), Mount Shasta, CA, USA.

Audios of Trigueirinho Lectures with simultaneous English translation

During over thirty years as Founder of the Figueira Community of Light, Trigueirinho gave bi-weekly lectures (called 'parthilha's or 'sharings') that were recorded live. Audience members were invited to submit questions to him which were placed in a small box and brought to him by an attendant. Arriving early, Trigueirinho sat at the lectern, reading through and taking notes on the audience questions. Thus, his lectures often began with the phrase "someone has asked a question...." After addressing some of these questions, he continued with the theme chosen for the day.

Approximately 70 of these 'sharings' were later dubbed with English translations. His voice or the translators can be augmented or diminished by adjusting the right-left balance of the recording.

To access these audio recordings go to the Shasti Association website:
www.shasti.org/instruction drop down the menu tab titled "Trigueirinho Instruction" and then click on "MP3 audios"

A Book to Be Written
A New Viewpoint of the Monad
Alopathic and Homeopathic Medicine
An Esoteric Dimension of Power
An Overview of Current Life
Angels and Humanity – 1
Angels and Humanity – 2
Angels and Humanity – 3
Angels and Humanity – 4
Bases of the Fiery World
Beyond Fire by Friction
Beyond Imperfection
Causal Body
Colors in Healing and the Formation of Our Light Vessel
Deep Healing
From the Human Kingdom to the Spiritual Kingdom
Getting through Today's Critical Times
Harmonization and Androgyny
How One Begins to Perceive One's Inner Self
How to Understand the Planetary Disasters
Human Trials | The Trials of the Soul
Information on the New Earth and the New Humanity
Inner and Outer Figueira
Instruction: a Step beyond Teaching
Liberating and Healing through Colors
Life in Cosmic Signs
New Supraterrestrial Pathways – 1
New Supraterrestrial Pathways – 2
New Supraterrestrial Pathways – 3
New Supraterrestrial Pathways – 4
Niskalkat

Noah's Vessel
On Vitality
Our Response to the Cosmos – 1
Our Response to the Cosmos – 2
Our Response to the Cosmos – 3
Our Response to the Cosmos – 4
Our Response to the Cosmos – 5
Our Response to the Cosmos – 6
Preparation for the Path of Initiation
Reflections on Illusion and Rescue
Reflections on Inner Attunement
Seeds of Inner Transformation
Seeking to Understand the Self
Several Levels of Spiritual Reading
Special Paths and the Path of the Majority
Spiritual Entities and Hierarchies
Spiritual Trials
Strengthening the Bases for the New Cycles
Subtle Bodies and Templing
Supraterrestrial Pathways – 1
Supraterrestrial Pathways – 2
Supraterrestrial Pathways – 3
Supraterrestrial Pathways – 4
Syntheses, Struggles and New Instructions
Taking Charge of One's Process of Dying – 1
Taking Charge of One's Process of Dying – 2
Taking Charge of One's Process of Dying – 3
The Art of Living in Current Times
The Cosmic Signs Reveal the Teaching – 1
The Cosmic Signs Reveal the Teaching – 2
The Desert
The Earth – Degeneration and Deliverance

The Era of the Gigantic Wave
The Importance of Self-Control in Epidemics
  and Other Risk Situations
The Light That Permeates Matter
The Mystery of the Cross in the Present
  Planetary Transition
The Doorways of the Planet – 1
The Doorways of the Planet – 2
The Doorways of the Planet – 3
The Doorways of the Planet – 4
The Doorways of the Planet – 5
The Days of Tomorrow
The Heart, the Ego and the Personality
The New Life That is Emerging
The Plan of Evolution and Us
The Practical Mystic
The Seventh Ray and the Devas
The Spark from the Divine Level
The Transmutation of the Logos of the Earth
The Voice of Amhaj
To Be Universal – Part 1
To Be Universal – Part 2
To Medical Doctors and Therapists
To Those Who Pray – 1
To Those Who Pray – 2
Towards Self Consecration
We are Part of the Cosmos
Working Spiritually with One's Mind
Working with the Feminine Polarity
Working with the Rays